competitor intelligence

To

Steven

Best wishes and good
luck in the CI Jungle!

Andrew Pollard

competitor intelligence

• • • • •

strategy, tools and
techniques for
competitive advantage

ANDREW POLLARD

FINANCIAL TIMES
PITMAN PUBLISHING

FINANCIAL TIMES

MANAGEMENT

LONDON · SAN FRANCISCO
KUALA LUMPUR · JOHANNESBURG

*Financial Times Management delivers the knowledge,
skills and understanding that enable students,
managers and organisations to achieve their ambitions,
whatever their needs, wherever they are.*

London Office:
128 Long Acre, London WC2E 9AN
Tel: +44 (0)171 447 2000
Fax: +44 (0)171 240 5771
Website: www.ftmanagement.com

A Division of Financial Times Professional Limited

First published in Great Britain in 1999

© Financial Times Professional Limited 1999

The right of Andrew Pollard to be identified as author
of this work has been asserted by him in accordance
with the Copyright, Designs and Patents Act 1988.

ISBN 0 273 63709 6

British Library Cataloguing in Publication Data
A CIP catalogue record for this book can be obtained from the British Library.

10 9 8 7 6 5 4 3 2 1

Typeset by Northern Phototypesetting Co Ltd, Bolton
Printed and bound in Great Britain by Bell & Bain Ltd, Glasgow

The Publishers' policy is to use paper manufactured from sustainable forests.

About the Author

Andrew Pollard is director and senior partner of EMP Intelligence Service and one of the most experienced consultants in competitor intelligence in Europe. His main areas of expertise lie in setting up practical competitor intelligence systems and in integrating competitor intelligence into the strategy of a business.

He has advised many companies in the UK, continental Europe, North America, the Middle East and South Africa. He also has vast experience in designing and running practical successful workshops in competitor intelligence and over 3500 managers have attended his workshops.

He has made presentations at many conferences on competitor intelligence and he has written a number of articles for the world's No 1 journal in competitor intelligence, *Competitive Intelligence Review*.

In 1987 the Open University in the UK published a pioneering multi-media management course, largely written and researched by Andrew, which included significant material and research on competitor intelligence. A highly successful course, it was taken by about 10 000 students.

He may be contacted at EMP.
Telephone: +44(1)604-755005.
Email: apollard@emp-is.com.

Contents

❼ Security and ethics *191*

Acknowledgements

This book would never have been written without the contribution of four sets of people:

- clients and testers of this book
- staff at EMP Intelligence Service
- peers and competitors
- my family.

First, I would like to thank the 3,500+ people who have attended EMP's public or in-house workshops on competitor intelligence and the hundreds of consultancy clients we have served since EMP was founded in 1988. In particular I would like to thank the following who reviewed earlier drafts of this book: Catherine Fanthome, John Geach, Kate Hayes, Jon Kimber, Colin Marson, Neil Owen, Adrian Roebuck, Ken Rooks and Peter Varnish. They are not responsible for any remaining shortcomings.

Then there are the staff at EMP who have helped me at many stages along the twists and turns of developing a practical, commercial body of knowledge on competitor intelligence and analysis. Special thanks go to John Edmunds for the graphics and to Adrian Dulstan for his assistance in preparing the various drafts. I hope they all think it was worth it!

And I must not forget my peers in the consultancy profession – practitioners and consultants – who have stimulated me to develop practical tools to help competitor intelligence managers and to bring it altogether into a coherent and useful framework. I found the Society of Competitive Intelligence Professionals conferences in the early 1990s particularly stimulating and thought-provoking.

Lastly, but certainly not least, my sincere thanks go to my family, and especially to my wife. Their support in this and in other ventures has been vital.

Introduction

What will you get out of this book?

If you are a senior manager, this book will show how the performance of your business can be improved by appropriate investment in competitor intelligence and analysis and how to invest in competitor intelligence for maximum return.

If you are a competitor intelligence manager tasked with developing, improving or resuscitating a competitor intelligence operation, this book will show you how to be successful. It will show you what it takes to make a significant contribution to the business, a contribution which, moreover, will be recognised by your senior managers and by your colleagues.

After reading this book, you should be able to do the following:

- Focus your competitor intelligence operation in the best way.
- Use competitor intelligence to support the business operations.
- Decide what competitor intelligence will provide the best return for the business.
- Spread your investment in competitor intelligence so as to maximise value and minimise risk.
- Ensure that the right intelligence goes to the right people in the right way at the right time.
- Invest wisely in the right processes of collecting competitor information from the right sources in the right way.
- Choose the most efficient and effective methods of processing competitor information into competitor intelligence.
- Reduce the losses suffered by your business from leaks of valuable information to competitors.

Each chapter concludes with a summary of the chapter and is followed by a troubleshooting section which identifies common problems associated with developing and running a competitor intelligence operation and identifies briefly how to deal with them.

The sources of the ideas in this book

Most of the ideas in this book were developed in response to business problems and challenges, or were developed for public or in-house workshops which I have run. I would like to thank our many clients for the opportunities to research and develop new ideas. (No confidential material, it should be stressed, has been included in this book.)

Some of the ideas were developed for the first time in consultancy work in the late 1970s onwards and some were first published in 1987 in a university course produced for the Open University in the United Kingdom called *Managing in the Competitive Environment*. It was taken by about 10,000 students. That course included the first published research in the UK into the practice of competitor intelligence and analysis. Some ideas were further developed for another course produced for Coventry University.

Other ideas were stimulated through contact with practitioners and consultants, particularly at Society of Competitive Intelligence Professionals conferences.

Overview of this book

The first chapter examines what competitor intelligence is and what benefits it can bring to a business. It concludes with a warning that without a successful competitor intelligence operation, businesses will suffer intelligence failure. This can be very serious, even leading to the loss of corporate independence.

Chapter 2 looks at the key factors in setting up and running a successful competitor intelligence operation. These fall under 5Ps: plan, people, position, processes and performance.

The book continues with four chapters on key processes:

- intelligence requirements
- information collection
- analysing competitors
- producing and communicating the right intelligence products.

Chapter 3 examines the best ways of identifying intelligence requirements and the underlying questions which need to be asked:

- Who are your customers?
- Why do they want competitor intelligence?
- How would the competitor intelligence be used?
- What competitor intelligence do they need?
- When and how do they want competitor intelligence?

The chapter concludes with a discussion of the methodologies for identifying customer requirements.

Chapter 4 analyses the sources of competitor information:

- internal sources – inside your company
- competitor sources
- third-party sources – e.g. suppliers, customers, government.

Chapter 5 deals with analysis, which may be taken as covering all the various processes which competitor information can go through between collection and communication. The pattern of analysis should be appropriate for the purpose at hand. It is always wise to remember that the true objective of analysis is a decision. Even if that decision is to do nothing, at least for the time being, it means that inaction is a preferred and evaluated option rather than a result of unthinking inertia.

Chapter 6 looks at the communication of intelligence. What kind of intelligence products should you produce? And how should they be communicated? The trick is to avoid becoming a bespoke researcher for most of the company without the funds to accomplish it, and getting the right balance between giving key people what they want while satisfying others with a more standardised product. The chapter also looks at the ways in which competitor intelligence should actually be delivered to final users. It offers alternatives to contributing to paper mountains and to death by Email.

Chapter 7 takes a look at two interconnected areas: security and ethics. It is important to realise the dangers of sloppy security. While you are piling up the benefits resulting from a well-run competitor intelligence operation, your company may be losing even more benefits, not because of bugging and other forms of industrial espionage (which are not covered in this book) but as the result of telephone inquiries by so-called 'students' and the work of trash analysts who collect and analyse your paper waste.

Much is talked about ethical business behaviour. This book will give you the truth regarding methods of collection by business, based on one of the best archives in the world (if not the best). This information in this book has never been published elsewhere. It is a warning to all businesses about how vulnerable they may be.

Gaining advantage from competitor intelligence

Competitor intelligence: What is it? Why invest in it?

What is competitor intelligence?
Why invest in competitor intelligence?

The benefits of competitor intelligence

Using competitor intelligence for business advantage
Competitor intelligence in a recession
Corporate radar
Closing the intelligence gap
Improved thinking and attitudes leading to better
*   plans and decisions*
Allied Steel and Wire

What will happen if you do not invest in competitor intelligence?

The lesson of Forte
Competitor intelligence failure
Pearl Harbor: the commercial lessons

Future trends in tools, techniques and practices

Summary of Chapter 1

Troubleshooting

Competitor intelligence: What is it?
Why invest in it?

'In the end, the best informed wins.'
Benjamin Disraeli

What is competitor intelligence?

Competitor intelligence is the output of a systematic and legal process for the gathering and analysing of information about the current and potential competitors of a business. For instance, this output may consist of a competitor's current thinking, their intentions, actions or performance. It may concern some significant change in any of these aspects of a competitor's behaviour. Alternatively, it may consist of comparisons (e.g. prices, service levels, etc.) between competitors or between competitors and your business. The intelligence may also consist of an assessment of a competitor's relative strengths and weaknesses and an identification of competitive opportunities and threats.

> *'If you know your enemy and yourself, you will win every battle.*
> *If you know yourself, but not your enemy for every battle won, you will suffer a loss.*
> *But if you are ignorant of your enemy and yourself,*
> *You are a fool and certain to be defeated in every battle'*
> Sun Tzu

CASE ILLUSTRATION
Reducing the impact of a new entrant

Competitor intelligence can be used for long-term positioning or to fight a promotional battle with a new entrant. Alternatively, it can be used to help win a particular customer by providing an assessment of relative strengths and weaknesses. A chemical company faced a potential new entrant in its core market. It put together a small team which identified key items of intelligence it needed in order to neutralise the impact of the new entrant and, if possible, to damage and delay the new entrant as much as possible.

Initially uncertain how to deal with the potential new entrant, the company, following the receipt of competitor intelligence, was able to strike at the weaknesses of the entry strategy of the target company. As a result, it retained market share.

Competitor intelligence is part of the total environmental intelligence a company needs in order to make correct decisions. As markets become more global and competition gets more intense, there is an increasing awareness of the benefits of all aspects of environmental intelligence. *Today, business exists in the Age of Intelligence.*

There are several different kinds of intelligence which are important to a business, and which impact upon its strategies and which determine the extent to which it is able to achieve its objectives. (*See* Figure 1.1.)

Fig. 1.1 A company's total intelligence requirement

Three terms – competitor, competitive and business intelligence – are frequently used, and Table 1.1 shows their various components.

Table 1.1 Different forms of intelligence

Focus	Competitor intelligence	Competitive intelligence	Business intelligence
Competitors	✓	✓	✓
Markets		✓	✓
Customers		✓	✓
Suppliers		✓	✓
STEPP factors			✓

The focus of this book will largely be on competit**or** intelligence and analysis. There will, however, also be occasional references to other elements of competit**ive** intelligence and sometimes to STEPP factor intelligence. STEPP stands for sociological, technological, economic, political and physical environmental factors.

Why invest in competitor intelligence?

'For all I know there is someone down the road about to put the skids under my entire operation.'
Chief Executive Officer, UK manufacturing company

The strategies and tactics employed by a company to achieve competitiveness and profitability must be supported and guided by appropriate intelligence.

In both the selection of appropriate strategies and in their execution, good intelligence is absolutely vital. You must know your competitors' capabilities and intentions and identify where your plan of execution will be most vulnerable to competitor attack. Apart from identifying potential threats to successful implementation, competitor intelligence should also highlight potential opportunities to improve strategies or their implementation.

It is probably true that some companies do succeed without a formal system for competitor intelligence, relying on the intuition or judgement of a few people. But for most companies this is too great a risk to take, and a formal and efficient system is needed.

> 'If you are profitable but not competitive,
> You will live today but not tomorrow,
> But if you are competitive but not profitable,
> You will probably not live to tomorrow'

The purpose of this book is to outline the essential elements of such a system.

A number of trends have combined in recent years to increase the need for *systematic* systems of competitor intelligence:

- increasing competition
- increased size of markets (globalisation of markets)
- increased pace of change (e.g. by governments deregulating)
- increasing size of companies (e.g. from globalisation and acquisitions)
- greater access to information (e.g. the Internet, intranets and extranets)
- development of sophisticated search engines (e.g. Alta Vista)
- improvements in technology making decentralised systems possible
- greater knowledge of the benefits of competitor intelligence.

The purpose of setting up a competitor intelligence operation is not to collect information on competitors as such, but to help the business achieve its ultimate objectives of profitability, competitiveness and independence. Unless these objectives are kept clearly in mind all the time, competitor intelligence dissolves into a 'nice-to-have' support exercise producing vaguely useful intelligence. Such support exercises are not uncommon. Competitor intelligence operations which actually deliver real significant bottom-line benefits are the exception; and one of the principal reasons for this is the lack of focus on the bottom line.

We must therefore keep firmly in mind that competitor intelligence is not generated for its own sake but to support business decision-making. If you do invest wisely in competitor intelligence, it could be worth £30m in profits from making more good decisions and fewer bad ones, as Robert Flynn, Chief Executive Officer, Nutrasweet is on record as admitting.

USES OF COMPETITIVE INTELLIGENCE
- **Strategic planning**
- **Plan adjustment**
- **Early warning**
- **Sales promotion**
- **Strategy support**
- **Competitive action plans**
- **Key account management**

The benefits of competitor intelligence

The Duke of Wellington was never defeated. Asked for the secret of his success, he replied that: 'It was knowing what was going on on the other side of the hill better than most men'.

Using competitor intelligence for business advantage

In a competitive environment, survival goes to the fittest (as well as to the privil-eged and sheer lucky!). The fittest business possesses competitive advantage. Understanding what competitive advantage means and what needs to be done to achieve it can only be obtained with quality competitor intelligence.

An essential ingredient of competitive advantage is a knowledge of competitor opportunities and threats, and, equally important, a knowledge of the relative strengths and weaknesses of competitors in comparison to your business. How, for instance, can you seize an opportunity if you do not know it is there?

There are many ways in which competitor intelligence can be used to improve business performance. Here are some examples:

- Increase own sales.
- Reduce the sales of competitors.
- Obtain higher prices.
- Decrease own costs.
- Reduce competitors' profitability.
- Increase the costs of competitors.
- Improve defensive strategies.
- Identify joint venture or takeover opportunities.
- Maintain independence.
- Prevent leakage of information.

To illustrate some of these options, here are some case illustrations drawn from consultancy experience.

Identify 'me too' opportunities

A European bank suffers from a strategic disadvantage because most of its retail outlets are concentrated in one part of the region. This is a serious nuisance because the bank nurtures pan-European ambitions. It achieves this through a mixture of direct mail and sales (i.e. loans) through selected third-party channels.

The products it sells are carefully researched 'me-toos' which it launches very soon after another bank has pioneered a new product and which are better designed and make more money than the pioneers' products.

The bank uses competitor intelligence to monitor certain of its competitors who are noted for their innovation in new product development. As soon as any of these competitors launch a new product or product extension, the bank carries out intensive market research to identify the strengths and weaknesses of these new products.

It then launches its own products capitalising on its ability to follow another company's innovation rather than have to develop new products itself. It is a very successful strategy for the bank, for it offers high returns and low risk. As the managing director of the bank said: 'Pioneers get scalped. We're fast followers'.

Identify competitive gaps

A European manufacturing company aimed to increase its turnover (and profitability) by 50 per cent in three years by organic growth. Such growth, in a market which was not growing, can only come at the expense of other competitors. Two-thirds of this growth was obtained by identifying competitive gaps in key competitors' product portfolios, and then exploiting their relative advantage in these gaps.

It sounds very easy, but in practice it was not. (But then if good competitor intelligence was easy, it would probably not produce the big benefits it can provide.) The company in question produced thousands of variations of about six different types of product. Understanding all that complexity and making comparisons with competitors' offerings was very difficult. Even senior managers of many years' experience could not cope with the problem. It needed a specially developed computer program which generated the competitive gaps, together with key additional information about competitors.

The result? Armed with its intelligence targeting 'machine' it raised its turnover by £5m in the first two years.

Reduce the impact of new competitor products

No competitor intelligence operation can guarantee to pick up in advance all new product developments by existing or potential competitors. But it can ensure that news of a new launch is received as soon as possible. The top management of a Fast Moving Consumer

Goods (FMCG) company with a major global brand did not learn of a major new competitive product in one of its key markets until a full six weeks after the launch!

This intelligence failure was repeated twice in the next three months as competitor 'me too' products were launched in other markets. By now, the management were stung into taking action and investment in competitor intelligence began. This enabled senior management to judge the seriousness of the threat of a new brand to its own brand and avoid wasting management time on the non-starters. It also started to get early warning intelligence, which gave senior management more time to think out the best response and to snuff out competitive threats before they became serious.

Before that they had spent too much time, in the words of the managing director, 'running around like headless chickens'.

Decrease competitors' sales

Service company A, based in the UK, found itself increasingly aware of the growth of another service provider B in another European country. At first the board of A considered B to be hardly worth any attention. Their opinion was that B was small, their quality was not very good and their judgement was coloured by a touch of good old British arrogance.

Unfortunately for A, the other company grew and grew and started to eat into a small part of A's core market. And by this time, their quality was 'quite good'. At last, at a board meeting, A decided to spend some money finding out how to beat B rather than assuming B would lose anyway just because they were inferior.

Surprisingly, the intelligence on B revealed a strong company, well run and with strong management focus, though suffering from increasing cost pressures. The intelligence indicated two viable options: fight B with lower prices or negotiate a joint venture/takeover. Given the previous attitude of the management, guess which option they took?

Identify hostile strategies and improve defensive strategies

Many of the ex-public sector UK utilities at the time of their privatisation were sitting on near-monopoly positions. While they were aware that they were bound to lose market share, some were determined to hang on to their most profitable customers. They needed to monitor at the local level the promotional activities of their new competitors.

To do this, one utility set up a competitor intelligence system which collected information from local networks. This information was fed back to the competitor intelligence centre, collated, analysed and transmitted to the marketing director on a weekly basis. With this information the marketing director was able to adjust his own promotional plans to take advantage of competitors' mistakes, learn from their innovative promotional ideas and neutralise competitors' efforts where it was in the utility's self-interest to do so.

Competitor intelligence in a recession

The need for competitor intelligence and analysis becomes greater in a recession when the size of the market ceases for a time to grow and business becomes more 'dog eat dog'. Taking market share from competitors requires competitor intelligence. In addition, in a recession acquisition opportunities at bargain prices become available – to those who know they are there.

A recession can also offer opportunities to weaken competitors as long as your company has previously invested in understanding their weaknesses. Work out what they should do in response to a recession and wait for a mistake. When the market downturn actually occurs, you are ready to take advantage of any ill-advised actions by competitors reacting hastily, in panic or without careful consideration.

CASE ILLUSTRATION

'There are none so blind as those who will not see.'

The marketing director of a transport company was bemoaning the fact that a major competitor had got into difficulties in a recent recession and before he became aware of the fact, the company had been purchased by one of his arch-competitors. Despite this obvious failure, he went on illogically to state that he saw no reason for an on-going competitor intelligence and analysis operation.

Lesson: Senior managers who want the benefits of knowing without investing in a good competitor intelligence and analysis operation will continue to weep over their ill-fortune rather than blame themselves.

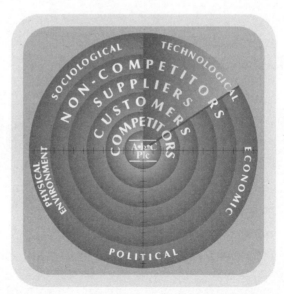

Fig. 1.2 Corporate radar sweeps the business environment

Corporate radar

Unfortunately senior managers are frequently blind to significant competitive movements. What they need is a kind of current and future 'corporate radar', which helps them to be made aware of significant changes in their competitive environment (see Figure 1.2). Competitor intelligence will do that. In particular, it will significantly improve the answers to the following questions:

- 'What significant activity is *currently occurring* in the competitive environment?'
- 'What significant activity is *going to happen* in the competitive environment in the future?'

Decision makers need to be made aware of current opportunities and threats and be able to anticipate them in the future. With this increased awareness decision makers can take appropriate offensive or defensive action:

- to improve its defence against competitor and other environmental threats
- to improve its capability to take advantage of competitive and other environmental opportunities.

Smaller companies need 'radar' as well as larger ones. Take, for instance, a company called Audience Systems, a company based in Wiltshire, England, employing about 50 people making specialist telescopic seating for sports halls, television studios and theatres. Their marketing director feels strongly that competitor intelligence is vital to the success of the company:

'It's very important, it's essential, that we know exactly what our competitors are doing all the time … We can't have enough of that type of information – in particular, information on product range, prices, order book, technical developments and marketing.'

Closing the intelligence gap

From the moment the size of a business grows beyond the ability of key decision makers to study their competitors themselves, that business must fill the intelligence gap which has opened up. This gap exists whether decision makers believe it exists or not. It's just hard business reality. And it must be filled. If 'nature abhors a vacuum', then it is equally true that a business abhors an intelligence vacuum. Like it or not, that gap fills. Either the intelligence gap is filled by evaluated intelligence or it fills itself with either of the following:

- conscious opinion based on judgement, guesswork or sheer speculation: *'I know or I think I know'*
- passive assumptions: *'I know I probably do not know. I'll fill the gap with assumptions'* or *'I'll just rely on others to do the work for me'*.

Relying for the most part on opinions or assumptions or both as the major methods of closing intelligence gaps can cause serious intelligence failures. Judgement alone is fine – as long as the decision makers really do know what they are doing and their intuition for the reality of markets and competitors does not seriously fail them. The problems with guesswork, assumptions and uninformed speculation are obvious. Blind decision making is the foundation stone for all kinds of disasters.

The best way of filling intelligence gaps is a systematic and ordered approach to identifying these gaps and then filling the important gaps with evaluated information collected in the right way from the right sources. Even the best decision makers admit (in private sometimes) that, while they rely a great deal on their own abilities, they do need information, if only to add weight to their own judgements.

CASE ILLUSTRATION
....
An FMCG company with a leading brand only collected competitor intelligence when they had to do so for the purposes of producing

annual revisions to the business plan. One consequence was that the quality of these revisions was reduced significantly. For instance, it was faced with responding to a significant economic recession in one of its country markets. In deciding how it should respond, the company had little or no information on the likely reactions of competitors to the recession and to any actions which it might take. Two pieces of information it needed were an analysis of competitor behaviour in previous recessions and an assessment of probable competitor reactions.

By not systematically filling its intelligence gaps another disadvantage the company suffered from was its inability to avoid knee-jerk reactions to competitor moves. It found it difficult to distinguish competitors' mistakes from their successes and important moves from unimportant moves. As a result it wasted a great deal of management time trying to work out whether and how it should respond to competitor moves.

The chief executive finally decided that an orderly process of collection and analysis of competitor intelligence was required. He arranged a series of brainstorming exercises among his key managers to highlight the crucial gaps and to set up the intelligence exercise.

Improved thinking and attitudes leading to better plans and decisions

'Good intelligence is an antidote for wishful thinking' said Winston Churchill. It introduces objective standards into the corporate thinking process and it also brings a wider source of ideas. Competitor intelligence is an aid to the experience, skill, intuition and gut feeling of managers. It can help a company discover best practice situations. Competitors can be viewed in part as sources of ideas.

Competitor intelligence also changes attitudes. It can make individuals more outward orientated and less insular, and as a result it can indirectly facilitate change. (That is why managers of competitor intelligence are also managers of change.)

Business objectives are more likely to be achieved if the right strategies are formulated and implemented. Identifying the right strategies, and adjusting them in the light of circumstances, are both significantly more likely with good competitor intelligence.

Allied Steel and Wire

A good case illustration of the importance of competitor intelligence and analysis is Allied Steel and Wire (ASW), a company based in Cardiff. This example shows just how crucial, how significant competitor analysis can be.

Alan Cox, head of ASW, reckons that competitor analysis was 'a pretty basic piece of work that companies ought to do'. When Cox took over, ASW was losing around £2m a month. Despite this Cox spent more than £1m on competitor analysis in the next 12 months. He argued that he wanted to 'see as many pieces around in the game' as he could. In his view there was no alternative to carrying out competitor intelligence and analysis.

One of the results of the competitor analysis was the discovery that ASW faced many more competitors than they had previously believed existed. ASW also put a lot of effort into relating their standards of performance against as many of these competitors as it could, in particular costs of production.

By finding out competitors' equipment and product mix, ASW built up potential costs for their competitors which could be adjusted according to assumptions about productivity. Other areas for analysis included how companies compared in terms of the products they produced.

This enabled ASW to identify the main areas of advantage in terms of product mix and exploit them, and those areas of its operations which require capital expenditure. The competitor analysis exercise at ASW goes on all the time. Thorough overhauls to the analysis are interspersed by more frequent revisions.

According to Cox competitiveness necessitates competitor analysis and without it you are not in control of your company. You are merely reacting to changes which suddenly hit the company out of the blue. He summed up his attitude to competitor intelligence and analysis as follows:

> *'I actually believe if you are making things that fundamental to being on the pitch, to being able to play the game, you have to have competitive costs on an ongoing basis. You have to know what that means, therefore you have to have objective standards, therefore you have to measure your competition against it and if you haven't got that, you shouldn't come out of the dressing room to play the game.'*
>
> Alan Cox, Chief Exective Officer, ASW

What will happen if you do not invest in competitor intelligence?

The lesson of Forte

In a competitive environment, competitor intelligence is not a 'nice-to-have'; it is a 'must-have'. Not having a good competitor intelligence operation can sometimes be lethal. At worst you could lose a lifetime's work as Forte did in 1995 when Granada won a hostile takeover battle against the Forte family and their shareholder supporters. Forte, the largest hotel chain in Europe, had been built up over 60 years by Lord Forte, but were caught napping by a smarter, quicker adversary that had apparently spent two years stalking Forte. Granada won the intelligence battle and Forte suffered a fatal intelligence failure.

Competitor intelligence failure

Companies are faced with the ever-present threat of intelligence failure. Intelligence failure occurs when, because of the ignorance of significant pieces of competitor intelligence, a company misses an important opportunity or suffers from an unforeseen threat. An unforeseen threat could emerge if a significant change in a company's relative strengths and weaknesses has taken place.

The lack of good competitor intelligence may seriously affect a company's performance in terms of competitiveness and profitability, even if the effect of intelligence failure is not so catastrophic as that which hit Forte.

From research carried out by EMP Intelligence Service, the major intelligence failures suffered by companies are as follows:

Opportunities missed
- Acquisition
- Competitors' launch problems
- Late delivery
- Joint ventures
- Ability to acquire key accounts

Threats unforeseen
- Joint ventures
- Market entry
- New products
- Price changes

Many managers are ignorant of the concept of intelligence failure but ignorance is no shield from suffering its damaging effects. *Unless managers do something to prevent intelligence failure they are condemned to suffer from it.* Hard as it may seem, companies in competitive environments have little option but to invest in competitor intelligence.

Companies which do not have a formal competitor intelligence operation because they do not think such a function would be useful, will still suffer intelligence failure. Good competitor intelligence brings business benefits. A poorly run competitor intelligence operation or no competitor intelligence at all weakens the business, sometimes significantly. The impact will ultimately be on the company's competitiveness, profitability and independence.

This failure may refer to the current situation or to a forecast situation. The impact of intelligence failure on the business, whether caused by plain ignorance or misconceptions, could be severe if the failure affects crucial actions or decisions.

All companies suffer to some degree from intelligence failure, whether they are aware of it or not. What matters is the extent of the intelligence failure. (A further examination of the causes and types of intelligence failure appears in Chapter 2.)

The only conclusion

If your business has competition, you must have an effective competitor intelligence operation. Being customer focused and customer aware is vital, but so, too, are competitor intelligence and analysis.

Competitor intelligence is vital for the success of a business. It is an essential ingredient in the development and execution of successful business strategies. Companies with successful competitor intelligence operations gain additional competitive advantage over their competitors.

Fortunately for those that do invest wisely in competitor intelligence, many companies still do not invest in competitor intelligence at all or else do so badly. *This book is for those managers who want to gain the benefits of a successful competitor intelligence operation.*

Pearl Harbor: the commercial lessons

We can learn a great deal from intelligence failures such as Pearl Harbor, because they are so well documented. Let us quickly remind ourselves of the background.

Between 07.55 and 09.45 on Sunday morning 7 December 1941, 360 Japanese planes attacked airfields and naval ships at anchor in Pearl Harbor without any warning. Eighteen United States ships, including some of the biggest ships in the US navy, were lost, 188 planes were destroyed and 3435 officers and men were killed and wounded. It was a massive intelligence failure.

At the end of the war, in 1945, Secretary of War Henry L Stimson appointed Major Henry C Clausen as the independent prosecutor to investigate the root causes of the disaster. He interviewed 92 of the most important players under oath and his report succeeded in identifying the causes of the debacle where other previous investigations were less successful. He also named names and his report assigned responsibility, which was one of the reasons why the report remained secret for so long. The following analysis is based on this book.

Clausen's report identified intelligence failure both in Washington and in Hawaii. In Washington the failure centred on the communication – or rather the lack of it – of decrypts of the Japanese diplomatic 'purple' code from the decrypters to senior military and government decision makers. (Since September 1940 the Army Signal Intelligence Service under Wolf Friedman had been able to decrypt the Japanese diplomatic 'purple' code. Between the beginning of 1941 and the attack on 7 December, the decrypters had decoded about half of the messages sent between Tokyo and Washington. While the decrypting itself was a technical breakthrough, the organisation of the decrypting and the communication of the decrypts were a shambles with the army and navy sharing responsibility.)

Clausen identified those responsible for communication at the decrypting operation as the main culprits – Colonel Rufus S Brattan and his assistant, Colonel Carlisle C Dusenbury. Brattan as the superior officer failed to ensure that his orders to Dusenbury to communicate the decrypts were actually carried out; and the fault of

Dusenbury was that he failed to do what he was told to do. The result was that nine valuable hours were lost between the decrypts being ready and the senior decision makers receiving them.

In Pearl Harbor, the largest measure of responsibility, according to Clausen, rested with Admiral Husband E Kimmel, Commander in Chief, US Pacific Fleet and Lt General Walter C Short, Commanding General, US Army, Hawaii. Short failed to respond to warnings from Washington, failed to carry out reconnaissance as he was told and failed to liaise with the navy in Pearl Harbor. Kimmell, for his part, withheld vital intelligence from Short.

The main causes of the Pearl Harbor intelligence failure were therefore:

- hoarding of information by the navy
- poor co-operation between army and navy
- slow communication of decrypts in Washington
- split responsibility between army and navy for decrypting and communicating intelligence
- lack of willingness to take action.

The commercial lessons of Pearl Harbor are startlingly clear. The root cause of the failure was not technical and did not lie in the collection of information. In fact, the decoding of the 'purple' code was a technical and intellectual triumph. Instead, the failure was human and centred on the following:

- lack of co-operation between relevant agencies
- low standards of performance
- poor supervision of others
- split responsibility
- inadequate reaction to information received.

As we shall see, these same human inadequacies are some of the key reasons which can prevent competitor intelligence operations from achieving their full potential. *One of the main objectives of this book is to reduce intelligence failure and to increase intelligence success.*

By way of a postscript, one reason for the Pearl Harbor failure which has not yet been mentioned was the low weight given to intelligence work and the effect this had on the operation. At the time of Pearl Harbor, intelligence was not the career for the thrusting, clever and ambitious young officer. Combat units in the armed forces were held in much higher regard by young officers carving out their career. As a result the intelligence unit got the duffers.

There are lessons for us today:

- Organisations are only as good as the people in them.
- Make sure the competitor intelligence function has status, otherwise the calibre of managers attracted to it will be low.
- Put people into competitor intelligence who understand the business and who have a successful track record.
- Make sure communication to decision makers is both prompt and effective.
- Do not assume senior decision makers know or will necessarily understand what is given them.

What you have to do for the competitor intelligence operation to be successful is the subject of the next chapter.

Future trends in tools, techniques and practices

After 15 years or so, since its modern reincarnation, competitor intelligence is beginning to develop a practical body of principles and processes. This will help it to be better understood by senior managers and to make the average competitor intelligence operation more successful.

In the next five years competitor intelligence will further integrate itself into business strategic and tactical thought and practice. Decision making in the real world is frequently made in ignorance and with fragmentary information about business conditions, including those relating to competitors. Business strategy and intelligence strategy need to be run side by side if companies are to take at least neorational decisions. In the future, success in business will increasingly go to senior managers who know how to use competitor intelligence.

From the collection point of view, the advent of the web browser interface and the growth of useful websites on the Internet is revolutionising the collection of external competitor intelligence. And with the growth of intranets, competitor intelligence managers will have at their terminals a 'one stop shopping' gateway to an enormous world of electronic information.

This is, of course, a double-edged sword and while it will make access to information easier, it will also raise the importance of good training to prevent massive information overload leading to muddle and confusion.

At the same time, the rise of knowledge management offers competitor intelligence managers an opportunity to capitalise on the skills they have developed. Despite some confusion over the meaning of knowledge management, the additional emphasis on 'knowledge' inside the company and the importance of tapping it and sharing it is a very important trend which competitor intelligence managers must take advantage of.

What is the most exciting prospect is the development of tools and processes which will both improve business strategy and sharpen the way competitor intelligence is used. It is to aid that development that this book was written.

Summary of Chapter 1

- Competitor intelligence is the systematic collection of relevant information about competitors and is a vital management tool in a competitive environment.

- Competitor intelligence varies from identifying a competitor's current and forecast activities to assessing its strengths and weaknesses and associated competitive opportunities and threats.

- Its use varies from supporting corporate decisions and strategies to supporting a salesperson attempting to close a deal.

- In a competitive environment companies need to invest in competitor intelligence so that they can improve their competitiveness and profitability and retain their independence.

- The main benefits of competitor intelligence lie in its support of a business's profitability and competitiveness and in improving decision making, planning and how it implements its decisions and plans.

- A good competitor intelligence operation will help to improve the culture of the company and improve teamwork.

- Businesses which do not invest in competitor intelligence will suffer intelligence failure, which can seriously damage a company's profitability and competitiveness, and can even threaten its corporate independence.

- The demand for competitor intelligence will grow and become more global.

Troubleshooting

Common problems	How to deal with them
Ignorance of the benefits of good intelligence and of the costs of having poor competitor intelligence or no intelligence at all	Educate and convince key decision makers and opinion formers
Significant errors in a company's understanding of its competitive environment and its relative position in it	Produce and implement a coherent and credible competitor intelligence plan and implement it

How to set up a successful competitor intelligence operation

Key success factors – overview

Plan: devise the right competitor intelligence strategy

Target intelligence versus radar/awareness intelligence
Expressed requirements versus own assessments
Producing for customers versus producing for suppliers
Tapping internal sources versus tapping external sources
Information versus intelligence
'Facts' versus rumours
Efficiency versus effectiveness

People: get the right people into competitor intelligence

Right people, right skills
Motivation to produce what customers want and need

Position: make competitor intelligence an important function in the business

Integrate competitor intelligence into the business
Senior management support and involvement

Processes: do things the right way

Accurate analysis of the internal market for competitor intelligence
Tap the right sources
Use the right storage and retrieval and production processes
Produce tailored, targeted intelligence products

▶

Performance: keep your eye on the ball

Measure and publicise the success of competitor intelligence
The key success factors of three companies

Avoiding intelligence failure

Input failures
Output failures
Process failures
The Tet offensive, South Vietnam 1967
SmithKline Beecham Consumer Healthcare overcomes the
* 'blockers'*

Summary of Chapter 2

Troubleshooting

Key success factors – overview

'The excellent companies clearly do more and better competitor analysis than the rest.'
Peters and Waterman

What *must* go right if a competitor intelligence operation is to succeed? Experience suggests the following key success factors.

The 5 Ps of competitor intelligence

Plan
- Devise the right competitor intelligence strategy.

People
- Get the right people into competitor intelligence.
- Motivate staff to produce what customers require.

Position
- Ensure senior management involvement and support.
- Integrate competitor intelligence into the business and support key decisions.

Processes
- Undertake an accurate analysis of internal market for competitor intelligence.
- Tap the right sources.
- Build a human network of sources.
- Use the right storage and retrieval and production processes.
- Produce the right, tailored and targeted intelligence products.
- Develop intelligence management and communication skills.

Performance

- Measure the performance of competitor intelligence.
- Obtain feedback from key customers.

Each of these key success factors is examined below.

Plan: devise the right competitor intelligence strategy

> *'The right information collected from the right sources, processed in the right way using the right techniques and communicated to the right people in the right manner at the right time – who then analyse it in the right way and take appropriate action.'*

The benefits of competitor intelligence can only be maximised with the right competitor intelligence strategy, which might be summarised in a mission statement for the competitor intelligence operation. Each company must determine its own most appropriate strategy for competitor intelligence. While each strategy will differ from the next, they should all include the following common components:

- what intelligence should be produced and for whom
- from what sources of information
- by what processes.

Within each of these components a number of balances must be struck between alternatives. These are set out below.

Target intelligence versus radar/awareness intelligence

A good competitor intelligence strategy should strike the right balance between target intelligence and radar/awareness intelligence.

Target intelligence is produced to pursue specific objectives or to support individual decisions. For instance:

- corporate strategic planning
- research and development decision making
- sales and marketing plans
- new product launches
- market entry
- acquisitions/mergers.

Target intelligence may be used in an offensive way (e.g. to gain a competitor's customer) or in a defensive way (e.g. to block entry into one's own market).

Radar/awareness intelligence is focused on key competitors and is concerned with knowing 'what's going on out there'. This form of competitor intelligence is very much like 'panning for gold' because it involves collecting information on competitors and sifting the information for nuggets. It is probably the most common form of competitor intelligence. Many senior managers, for instance, want an ongoing tailored news service on competitor activity. The challenge facing a business is to produce radar/awareness intelligence cost-effectively and to give managers what they require without collecting vast amounts of information.

A radar/awareness intelligence strategy emphasises the continuous production of competitor intelligence in order to identify significant changes in the competitive environment which might affect:

- current and future relative competitive strengths and weaknesses
- current and future competitive opportunities and threats (including obtaining advanced warning of competitor moves).

Getting the balance right between target intelligence and radar/ awareness intelligence is most important. It is all too easy to spend most of the competitor intelligence budget on published news inputs (usually electronic). Companies that do this are making a great mistake. Supporting specific decisions or strategies with targeted intelligence collection is usually going to produce a more obvious return on the investment than the money on spent awareness. Nevertheless, to get the best overall return on the investment in competitor intelligence, you need both radar awareness intelligence as well as target intelligence.

Expressed requirements versus own assessments

Another tension to be resolved in the intelligence strategy is that between intelligence requirements as expressed by a customer and the competitor intelligence manager's own estimates of the customer's real requirements. While it is important for a competitor intelligence operation to be customer driven, customers do not always know what they need, though many think they do!

Even if they do know what they need at the moment and can express it clearly, they may not forecast their future needs correctly. A competitor intelligence manager has to balance satisfying expressed requirements against perceived real needs and future requirements.

Producing for customers versus producing for suppliers

A balance has to be achieved between producing intelligence for decision makers only, many of whom will be senior managers with control over the competitor intelligence budget, and producing intelligence both for decision makers and for potential internal sources in return for their co-operation. As you will see later in the book a key success factor for competitor intelligence operations is the building of an internal network. One way of building up such a network is to provide key potential sources with information which may be useful to them.

Tapping internal sources versus tapping external sources

One of the big decisions in developing a competitor intelligence strategy is to establish the correct balance between tapping internal and external sources. Many of the latter, particularly electronic sources, are tempting to use to excess because of their ease and convenience. However, competitor intelligence managers must resist the temptation to spend all their budget on external electronic sources. *The most useful sources of competitor information frequently lie inside the company and not outside.*

Information versus intelligence

There is a difference between information and intelligence. Intelligence is added-value information. Another way of thinking about it is to think of intelligence as evaluated information. There is a market in every company for both information and intelligence, and a good competitor intelligence operation will balance the two according to the needs of the company. This particular tension will be examined in more detail in Chapter 3 (pages 68–9).

Sometimes this particular debate is expressed as news versus analysis, for instance whether to reproduce or summarise press comment or whether to produce assessments of strengths and weaknesses.

'Facts' versus rumours

Managers must establish a balance between producing intelligence containing rumours and speculation and producing or supplying so-called facts only.

For instance, a senior manager might say *'I only want hard facts – no rumours'*. However, this division between rumours and speculation and so-called fact may often be more perceived than real. Where the line should be drawn between so-called facts and rumours depends on the type of competitor intelligence required by customers and on the ability of the competitor intelligence manager to collect and process rumours and to produce useful speculation. It also depends on the ability and willingness of customers to handle and use speculative information.

But it should be said quite bluntly: the manager who wants only 'facts' as, say, published in the *Financial Times*, but rejects trade rumours, or who is happy with published accounting information but rejects guesstimates of, say, plant capacity, is living in a strange world.

There are two other ways of classifying competitor information which can cause confusion:

- 'Hard' versus 'soft' information
- 'Quantitative' versus 'qualitative' information.

Published material may appear 'hard' or factual when frequently it is partial, outdated and sometimes simply inaccurate. To call statistics and financial statements 'hard' and opinion and commentary 'soft' makes little real sense. Indeed, it is good advice to avoid the hard/soft distinction altogether.

The distinction between qualitative and quantitative information is another one fraught with ambiguity. For instance, a press report stating that a competitor intends reducing capacity by 20 per cent contains quantitative information. But that figure of 20 per cent may in fact be an average of two different opinions or rumours or it may be the personal judgement of the reporter.

As they say, there are lies, damned lies and statistics ... and also accounting information! It is wise to treat all kinds of information as just raw information and to classify it simply by date, subject, source and perceived accuracy. We shall look further at this area on pages 127–8 in Chapter 5).

Efficiency versus effectiveness

'There's no sense in having a great system which doesn't produce the right stuff.'
Competitor intelligence manager

Competitor intelligence managers must achieve a balance between efficiency and effectiveness. **Efficiency** means collecting and producing intelligence in the right way whereas **effectiveness** means producing the right competitor intelligence at the right time. If the emphasis in a competitor intelligence operation is on news production (i.e. radar/awareness intelligence), then efficiency in the gathering and filtering of large amounts of competitor information will be important. But if target intelligence work is most important, the emphasis will be more on effectiveness.

> **EFFECTIVE COMPETITIVE INTELLIGENCE**
> - Know what business decisions are being taken.
> - Anticipate major future business decisions.
> - Know how competitor intelligence will be used.
> - Develop a competitor intelligence use plan to identify:
>   - what is relevant
>   - who should use it and how
>   - how to monitor use.

The balance between efficiency and effectiveness obviously has implications for resource allocation within the competitor intelligence operation, including the management of the competitor intelligence manager's time. Target intelligence work is frequently more demanding in terms of time than dealing with news, because more analysis is involved.

People: get the right people into competitor intelligence

Right people, right skills

Competitor intelligence needs the right people or it will fail. What are needed are people with good knowledge of the business and with strong communication skills, who are as good with the board as well as with the salesforce (and others too). They need to have courage (to tell the truth), diplomacy (to tell the truth tactfully), determination (to keep on telling the truth), and enough intellect to recognise the truth in the first place and to appreciate when they do not know or know incompletely, which is frequently the case.

Fig. 2.1 Key skills for competitor intelligence

A competitor intelligence manager must have skills in the following broad areas:

- managing internal customers
- managing information suppliers
- managing intelligence production processes.

Competitor intelligence managers must be prepared to develop a wide range of skills, from good organisational and project management skills to the managerial skills needed to tap internal sources.

They must master the skills of producing tailored intelligence and of communicating that intelligence in the most appropriate manner.

One of the biggest misconceptions in competitor intelligence work is to assume that you need lots of formal business qualifications (e.g. MBAs). In reality, competitor intelligence managers need to be 'jacks of all trades' possessing some skill in a variety of areas: knowledge of the business, leadership, management, diplomacy, education, writing, oratory, sales and marketing. In short, a competitor intelligence manager is not a specialist.

Some of these skills are 'guru' skills (e.g. financial analysis) but others, equally important, are interpersonal/people skills (e.g. presentation, interviewing). Above all, competitor intelligence operation managers need experience of the business, a strong preference for objectivity, 'warts and all', and an ability to market and sell the competitor intelligence operation.

It is important to promote *your* intelligence operation. Its success depends enormously on the skills of the competitor intelligence manager to market and sell the operation and its output. This form of sales and marketing is more akin to the sales and marketing carried out by a small business than that of a large corporation.

Sales skills are important as competitor intelligence managers must sell not only their operation but themselves and their intelligence. They are selling not only to customers but to suppliers of competitor information (e.g. sales) as well. In doing so competitor intelligence managers should try to brand their operations with a suitable logo and name. This gives the operation visibility and identity.

Table 2.1 indicates some of the individual skills needed to be efficient in the three areas already identified in Figure 2.1.

Table 2.1 Individual skills for competitor intelligence

Skills	Managing internal customers	Managing suppliers	Managing production
Sales and marketing	✓	✓	
Interviewing	✓	✓	
Workshops	✓	✓	✓
Intellectual	✓	✓	✓
Personal	✓	✓	✓
Template construction	✓		✓
Manual filing/ organisation			✓

Each of these skills will be discussed later. For now, they are briefly defined below:

Sales and marketing – the ability to market and sell competitor intelligence as a business benefit to others.

Interviewing – the ability to get intelligence requirements out of unwilling or ignorant senior managers and the ability to get sources of competitor information to speak.

Workshops – the ability to use group sessions in a variety of ways to help people to learn, make decisions and work together.

Intellectual skills – the ability to analyse and synthesise information to produce added-value insights.

Personal skills – the skills needed for effective rapport and communication with customers and suppliers.

Template construction – the ability to design clear, short but informative intelligence products which will actually be used by intelligence customers.

Manual filing/organisation – the ability to organise hard copy and electronic information in a way which is easy to understand and use.

Motivation to produce what customers want and need

You must have real drive to produce what customers want and need. To succeed in competitor intelligence managers must really want to satisfy their internal customers – satisfy them in terms of what they want (or say they want) and also in terms of what they are likely to need in the future. Competitor intelligence managers must research their customers to discover their underlying or future needs. Not only must they give them *what* they need but also *how* they need it.

It is crucial to develop a clear understanding of their needs as well as their articulated wants. Senior managers should be researched as assiduously as you would research an important segment of an external market, using a variety of sources and techniques. Try to forecast senior managers' needs in advance by identifying decisions before they need to be taken.

Unless otherwise instructed, focus your intelligence operations on the current and future needs of a limited number of senior managers. You cannot serve everybody unless you have been given the resources to do so. *Even if you have been given a wide brief you should focus initially on the requirements of senior managers and win their support.*

Position: make competitor intelligence an important function in the business

Integrate competitor intelligence into the business

The worst thing that can happen to a competitor intelligence operation is for it to become merely a somewhat detached support service unconnected to the mainstream activities of the company. If competitor intelligence is to add value fully to the business, it must be integrated into the lifestream of the organisation.

Being integrated means in the first place that the mission statement of the competitor intelligence operation must be based on the mission statement of the business or the business units it is serving. Second, it means that the competitor intelligence operation should be fully integrated with the business objectives and with their formulation. Competitor intelligence should be used to validate the assumptions behind the business plan and test the realism of the objectives in the business plan against competitors' strategies.

COMPETITOR INTELLIGENCE SHOULD BE INTEGRATED WITH:

- mission statement
- business objectives
- decision making
- business plans
- business processes
- key decision makers

Competitor intelligence can help to identify possible competitor responses so as to improve the ability of the business to achieve the objectives it has set. Without competitor intelligence, business plans are less likely to achieve their objectives.

Competitor intelligence should be integrated into the decision-making structure of the business, from the sales and marketing meetings to the board meetings of senior executives. Some of the key areas of the decision-making mechanism of the business are:

- strategic planning process
- capital allocation process
- budgeting process.

CASE ILLUSTRATION

Integration with the sales and marketing strategy

An FMCG company was experiencing rising sales but falling profitability as it found it had to cut margins to maintain volume. Although first in its market, the company was becoming increasingly fearful that its lead over other brands was being eroded. After a great deal of work a new sales strategy was formulated. Competitor intelligence was essential in the formulation of the strategy and in its execution.

In particular, the company was concerned how to recapture ground lost to a cheaper competitor in part of the United States market. It particularly wanted to assess the likely reaction of the competitor if it reduced the price of its product. Research indicated that the competitor would probably not respond to maintain its price differential. The implementation of the new pricing strategy led to a 15 per cent increase in volume sales.

Competitor intelligence should also be integrated with the more detailed basic processes in the business, such as:

- opportunity selection
  - market segmentation
  - targeting
- solution design
  - research and development
  - production
  - marketing
- solution delivery
  - customer relations
  - service levels
  - customer satisfaction surveys.

Finally, competitor intelligence should be integrated at the human level with key actual and potential users of competitor intelligence –

for example, those involved in strategy formulation and execution and those involved in sales.

Senior management support and involvement

Both support *and* involvement are need. Without both, the competitor intelligence operation will lack internal credibility and will be starved of its lifeblood – the feedback from senior customers for which the competitor intelligence has been produced. One indicator of senior management support is the ability to purchase quality equipment and specialist software without having to spend nine months arguing the toss in five Information Technology committees. (IT managers with little understanding of competitor intelligence are frequently a significant obstacle to a successful operation, just as a well informed IT manager can be a major boost.) Another indicator of senior manager support is to give the competitor intelligence operation its own budget.

Processes: do things the right way

Accurate analysis of the internal market for competitor intelligence

Knowledge of the marketplace is fundamental to the provision of any business product or service. The same applies to the provision of competitor intelligence. A rigorous analysis of the internal marketplace is needed to answer the following questions:

- What are the business needs?
- Who are your customers for competitor intelligence?
- Why do they want or need competitor intelligence?
- What competitor intelligence do these customers require?

● When and how do these customers require competitor intelligence?

It is important to analyse the best ways in which answers to the above questions can be obtained. Each of these questions will be examined in more detail in Chapter 3.

Tap the right sources

The pattern of sources should be chosen so as to achieve the maximum quality for the minimum cost (both time and money). High quality competitor intelligence requires a correct match of internal and external sources to the intelligence requirements. While external sources can be helpful, it is important not to waste a large amount of the budget on external database information. Most useful competitor intelligence frequently lies within the company in the minds of managers and in internal paper and computer files. It is therefore vital that internal sources are tapped, which means that a competitor intelligence manager must build a human competitor intelligence network.

Getting the right pattern of sources is also important because the pattern of sources determines the pattern and validity of the information obtained. The wrong pattern of sources will produce a distorted picture and will also affect the credibility of the picture. *The balance of sources should be chosen so as to provide corroboration in important areas*. Chapter 4 will provide more detail on internal and external sources.

Use the right storage and retrieval and production processes

Intelligence production, together with associated processes, may be likened to a machine producing a range of products from carefully selected raw materials. The quality of the output obviously depends on the clarity and appropriateness of requirements, and the quality of the inputs. But it also depends on the quality of the intelligence machine and associated processes and the people who operate it. Intelligence managers must know what they are producing, for whom and why, and they must also be efficient in production.

The production of intelligence should be organised to ensure that the final product is tailor-made to the customer and to ensure as much time for thinking and analysis as possible. It should be organised so as to produce intelligence on time. If intelligence production is cumbersome and slow, the time for thinking is reduced and is filled with clerical work. Putting into place the right competitor intelligence processes allows managers to continue to be managers and not become expensively paid clerks.

A critical intelligence process is that of communication or dissemination. Competitor intelligence must be communicated correctly or it is useless. What the word 'correctly' means depends on the circumstances and the personalities of the internal customers. (This is examined in more detail on pages 184–7.)

Produce tailored, targeted intelligence products

Customise your intelligence – but don't go too far. The intelligence product for an individual manager must be constructed specifically for that manager. It must not be a generalised mass of information, too long to be digested; nor must it be too difficult to read even if they have the time. You must find out what customers want. That is not to say that all intelligence products are tailored for only one person. Unnecessary variations are a waste of time and money.

Good competitor intelligence is customer driven. It is vital to work hard to tailor intelligence products to customer requirements which answer the 'so what' factor. It is also important that intelligence products are disseminated in the most appropriate ways, both in terms of form and channel.

If senior managers want their intelligence presented in the form of bullet points, present it in that way. If they want it on paper rather than on computer, give it to them. If you can present your intelligence in an oral presentation, so much the better. It need not be a long presentation but the personal contact will enable you to tune your efforts even more finely in the future. By hook or by crook, get feedback from your senior managers. The competitor intelligence manager must gain cultural acceptance and be respected.

Performance: keep your eye on the ball

Measure and publicise the success of competitor intelligence

'What gets measured gets managed.'

There are a number of ways in which the performance of a competitor intelligence operation can be measured:

- the quality of internal information collected
- its use by key decision makers and impact on decisions
- repeat business from key decision makers
- involvement in meetings
- speed of response to requests.

One way of measuring the success of a competitor intelligence operation is to assess the impact on decisions of the intelligence provided. Has the intelligence made any difference whatsoever? How and in what ways are decisions different because of the intelligence? Just how many action plans based on competitor intelligence were actually acted upon? One of the advantages of producing target competitor intelligence is that it is more straightforward to assess the impact of the intelligence.

The competitor intelligence operation must become the focal point in the organisation for competitor intelligence. Its staff must gain respect for their knowledge and vision of the market and the competitors. They will gain this respect by delivering good intelligence.

An effective competitor intelligence operation knows what business decisions are being taken, anticipates major future decisions and knows how the competitor intelligence that is collected will be used. It then customises intelligence outputs to decision makers and verifies that key competitor intelligence requirements are met. An efficient competitor intelligence operation carefully analyses the gap between what intelligence is needed and what intelligence the business already has. It develops a plan to identify from what sources the gap will be filled and how it will be analysed.

At the end of the day, the acid test for success would be the renewal of your competitor intelligence operation budget at the end of the financial year. Even better – getting an increase in budget because they just can't do without you – or rather your intelligence! Aim to become indispensable.

Although you should manage your competitor intelligence operation to be successful and measure your success according to the measures indicated above, that is not enough in the harsh world of business. You should make sure key people know you are successful. Publicise the operation's contribution to decision making and highlight your successes. You are your own public relations officer!

The key success factors of three companies

Here are evaluations of the competitor intelligence operations of three companies, all based in Europe. Each of the key success factors for each company is marked out of ten. The UK company was a large FMCG business with a turnover of £5000m and with a well-known household name. The US company operated in all the major countries of Western Europe with headquarters in the UK, where most of the top management were British. The French company was part of an international business and the figures below refer to that part of the business operating in France itself. (These measures, which are not normally shown to clients, are based on a subjective evaluation but grounded on a rigorous investigation of a company's competitor intelligence operation.)

Key success factor	UK	USA	France
1 Right competitor intelligence strategy	7	7	6
2 Senior management support and involvement	6	7	7
3 Competitor intelligence embedded in the business	5	3	4
4 Accurate analysis of internal market	5	3	5
5 Real drive to produce what is wanted	7	4	5
6 Tapping the right sources	6	5	5
7 Using the right processes	5	3	4
8 Tailored, targeted intelligence products	5	4	6
9 Intelligence management skills	4	5	4
10 Measuring the success of competitor intelligence	3	4	3
Total score (out of 100)	**53**	**45**	**49**

The UK company was quite good in many ways but still needed to raise its performance by 20 points in order to bring it up to a desirable level. Relatively strong areas were intelligence strategy and real drive to produce what was wanted. But overall, the UK company lacked firm commitment from senior management and the skills to deliver a really good product.

The US company suffered from the fact that they were experiencing competition for the first time. The top management (mainly British) wanted the intelligence but at first they did not want to invest adequately in competitor intelligence and analysis. They wanted the benefits but at bargain basement prices. (This is all too common.) All the same, there was a positive ending to the story. Three months after an initial dithering decision to invest but only if it was cheap the board made up their minds, realised what was at stake and shelled out the money. As a result measured ratings began to climb.

The French company scored quite well at the very top of the management pyramid. They were very clear-headed, knew what they wanted, accepted the need for competitor intelligence, and knew how they were going to use it. Unfortunately, their clarity was not transmitted downwards very far. The formal channels of communication, based on a rather paternalistic, hierarchical culture, made the development of the necessary processes for success straightforward in one way ('the top has decided') but in another ways, very difficult.

By way of a footnote, here is an object lesson of what can go wrong in a competitor intelligence operation. The company's score was an almost unbelievable 8, the lowest score ever calculated.

In this company, the two people with responsibility for the competitor intelligence operation were running a job-share exercise and were only in the building together on one day a week. (Shades of Pearl Harbor and divided responsibility!) For some reason, they were quite unwilling to ask internal customers what they wanted and produce what these customers wanted. They were simply providing abstracts of articles from the journals kept by the library, abstracts written by librarians with no business experience. No wonder the sales director observed that what he was currently receiving was 'not in a readily digestible form'. He also remarked that he had 'received nothing from the competitor team for 4–6 months'.

Yet ten seconds walk away from their offices, key account managers were 'dying' for good competitor intelligence. Some of them, too, had vast amounts of competitor information in their heads which were not being tapped. The only real remedy was to scrap the system and find new people.

Avoiding intelligence failure

'It is pardonable to be defeated but not to be surprised.'
Frederick the Great

The concept of intelligence failure was introduced in the last chapter on pages 18–22. It is time we looked more deeply at the different causes and types of intelligence failure because if you want to set up and run a successful competitor intelligence operation, you need to be aware of the pitfalls you could fall into.

Merely starting a competitor intelligence operation is no insurance against significant intelligence failure. Just as there are key **success** factors for competitor intelligence, there are also key **failure** factors.

Intelligence failure arising from poor management of the competitor intelligence operation can occur in one or more of the three components of intelligence work:

- input failures
- output failures
- process failures.

Input failures

- choosing the wrong targets
- selecting the wrong key intelligence requirements
- tapping the wrong sources
- collecting too much information
- poor filtering
- neglecting people skills
- not building up an internal network.

Output failures

- lack of senior management involvement or targeting the wrong managers

- producing the wrong intelligence product (in terms of volume, quality, appropriateness and timeliness)
- poor communication
- neglecting people skills.

Process failures

- poor storage and retrieval system
- inadequate analytical techniques
- too much or too little analysis
- inefficient intelligence production methods
- neglecting people skills
- inadequate feedback from customers.

If a company wishes to avoid intelligence failure, there are some important lessons to be learned, both by decision makers and by intelligence producers.

Above all, decision makers must be prepared to take action on the basis of intelligence which has been carefully produced for the purposes which they themselves have identified.

The Tet offensive, South Vietnam 1967

Let it not be said that competitor intelligence managers are illustrations of the old dictum: 'We learn from history that we do not learn from history'. We can learn from past intelligence mistakes. Otherwise we are condemned to repeat them.

For example, we can learn from an excellent piece of research into the intelligence failure associated with the massive surprise attack by the Vietcong and North Vietnamese regulars on American and South Vietnamese forces in 1967. It is based on a book by the American author James J Wirtz entitled *The Tet Offensive: Intelligence Failure in War*. At the time of writing Wirtz taught in the US Department of National Security Affairs at the Naval Postgraduate School.

First, some background. Over 30 years ago on the last day of January 1967, at around 03.00 local time, soldiers and guerillas of the North Vietnamese Army and the South Vietnamese Vietcong simultaneously attacked 140 South Vietnamese cities, provincial capitals and district towns.

The Tet offensive, as it was to be called, had been launched the previous evening by the broadcasting on Radio Hanoi of a poem written by Ho Chi Minh, the head of the North Vietnamese government:

The theatre of the Vietnam War

This spring far outshines previous springs.
Of triumphs throughout the land come happy tidings.
Forward! Total victory shall be ours!

The timing, scale, extent and co-ordination of the Tet offensive were not anticipated by most US intelligence officers and by senior command. As a result, US forces had suffered a serious, indeed fatal, intelligence failure.

This intelligence failure gave the communist forces the great benefit of surprise, from which flowed two immediate benefits – military gains and political shock. More significantly, the intelligence failure of the Americans ultimately gave the communists the longer-term benefit of the seizure of the whole of South Vietnam.

The consequences of intelligence failure

The Tet offensive and its associated intelligence failure was the turn-ing point in the Vietnam War. Yet in the short term it was a failure. First, it was a military failure. The military gains were short-lived and consumed large numbers of communist forces and resources. At Hue alone they lost around 5000 men.

Second, it was a short-term political failure. The main aim of the Tet offensive had been to stimulate a general uprising of the South Vietnamese people against the 'US and the Puppet regime' as com-munist propaganda put it at the time. But the South Vietnamese people did not rise up.

But where the political fallout was immense was not in Vietnam but in the USA itself. To quote from James Wirtz's book:

> 'By the time the offensive's intensity began to wane on 13 February, 1100 Americans had been killed in action, and members of the Johnson admin-istration and the American public had been stunned by the fury of the Tet attacks. ... The Tet offensive was the decisive battle of the Vietnam War because of its profound impact on American attitudes about involvement in Southeast Asia. In the aftermath of Tet, many Americans became disil-lusioned with the Johnson administration's conduct of the war.'

What went wrong?

The causes of the intelligence failure to predict the Tet offensive were numerous. *Certainly they were not to do with intelligence collection.* The Americans had lots of evidence that something big was coming up and several pieces of unequivocal evidence were in their hands before 31 January.

Nor did the bulk of the intelligence failures occur at the other end of the intelligence cycle – intelligence dissemination. True, there were problems in communicating a last-minute realisation to the various Allied armed forces in South Vietnam that a major offensive was imminent. But to be realistic, the intelligence at that time, though accurate, was no longer timely. The enemy was already at the gate and in some cases already within it.

No, the bulk of the failures took place in the area of intelligence analysis. Some of the main failures of analysis are summarised below.

First, pre-established beliefs, such as that communist forces would never attack during the truce called for the Tet religious holiday. This ignored several significant historical precedents where Vietnamese military operations had been initiated during the Tet holiday.

Second, incorrect analogies from the past. The US Command appeared to be overly influenced by the fear that they would make the same mistake at Khe Sanh, which was then being besieged by communist forces, as the French had made 13 years before at Dien Bien Phu. (It was, of course, the shattering defeat of the French at Dien Bien Phu in 1954 that led to the total withdrawal of the French from Indo-China.) A more correct analogy would have been the Battle of the Bulge in Europe during the Second World War, when a nearly defeated army launched a desperate last-ditch counterattack under conditions of great secrecy.

Third, the inability of the US intelligence analysts – and one must sympathise with them in this – to predict communist mistakes. For the Tet offensive was based, in the minds of the North Vietnamese politicians, on a totally incorrect assessment of the likelihood of the South Vietnamese population to join the offensive in popular upris-ings. The US intelligence analysts, knowing better the attitudes of the South Vietnamese population, viewed the captured documents predicting general uprisings in South Vietnam as wishful thinking. They just did not think the North Vietnamese politburo would ever believe the rosy reports coming out of the South. But they did.

Finally, the active deception by the communists, ranging from diversionary attacks at Khe Sanh and elsewhere, which fuelled the

Americans' fear of another Dien Bien Phu, to diplomatic lies and fabrications intended to encourage the Americans and others to think that the North Vietnamese were serious about possible negotiations.

Lessons to be learned for competitor intelligence

At this point, let us leave the military arena and events of over 30 years ago and instead turn our attention to intelligence failure today in the arena of competitor intelligence and analysis. One of the main lessons to be learned is that unwillingness to accept reality is a fundamental problem. So, too, are pre-established beliefs – a tendency to filter out unwelcome information. This has been called 'premature cognitive closure', which appears to mean 'I've made up my mind already'. The danger of having closed minds is that it encourages what may be called 'Intelligence to please' – giving intelligence customers what they will like.

One big UK company identified the solitary outlet of a US company in competition with one of its own outlets in this country. It was the first time the UK company had competed against the US company. And what were the reactions of the UK company? 'Oh, they're not really competition'. 'They won't be able to adapt their US approach to UK market conditions'. 'They can't make a profit – not the way they normally do things'. They were wrong. The US firm showed much more flexibility than was anticipated in pricing and in operational procedures. And what's more, they were doing well too.

SmithKline Beecham Consumer Healthcare overcomes the 'blockers'

Here is a story of a competitor intelligence operation which is a lesson for us all. It concerns the Consumer Healthcare part of SmithKline Beecham – the part that included oral, gastrointestinal, smoking control and nutritional products. With sales of nearly £2.5

billion and profits of about £400m SmithKline Beecham is the number one oral health company in Western Europe and number three in the world in over-the-counter medicines.

In 1991 a competitor intelligence operation was started in the research labs in Weybridge in the UK. As this was a success, a global competitor intelligence operation was begun for the whole of Consumer Healthcare. This, too, has proved to be successful but over the years it has had to overcome some problems. These problems were termed 'blockers' by the competitor intelligence managers in Consumer Healthcare.

They divided these blockers into three types:

- senior management
- excuses
- other.

Senior managers were understandably nervous about investing in the unknown, given the many demands on their resources. They found it difficult to imagine any payback from the apparently intangible nature of competitor intelligence. These blockers were overcome by using existing resources as far as possible and by winning support among middle and senior managers by pointing out that their competitors had invested in competitor intelligence.

Some 'blockers' were really excuses, such as worries about security issues, dislike of computers and a 'not invented here' syndrome. Other blockers were managers' unwillingness to share information and a lack of interest in anything that did not directly benefit individual managers. Anti-computer attitudes were overcome in part by providing easy-to-use software and by providing lots of training and online help. Other blockers were overcome by changing the culture. Above all, the competitor intelligence operation focused on the business needs and on customer requirements and was willing to keep reinventing itself to maintain its relevance.

Summary of Chapter 2

- The 5 Ps of competitor intelligence are:

  - **plan**

  - **people**

  - **position**

  - **processes**

  - **performance.**

- The two basic types of competitor intelligence are ongoing radar awareness intelligence and target intelligence.

- For competitor intelligence to be successful, it must be integrated into the business strategies and decision making, and also with key decision makers.

- Competitor intelligence managers need to be excellent communicators, good with people and have a range personal attributes and skills.

- A competitor intelligence operation can suffer intelligence failure for the following reasons:

  - input failures

  - output failures

  - process failures.

Troubleshooting

Common problems	How to deal with them
Low value added from competitor intelligence caused by incorrect balance between radar awareness and target intelligence	Identifying the best combination of radar and target intelligence
Supporting the right business strategies	Rigorous analysis of competing strategies with competitor intelligence
Radar intelligence covering too many targets or requirements	Correct assessment of competing intelligence targets
Intelligence operation not properly integrated into business operations	Integrate the competitor intelligence operation in decision making, plan formulation and with key decision makers
Competitor intelligence staff who lack key skills: interpersonal, project management and information handling Staff who lack innate abilities: determination, bravery and diplomacy	Carefully appoint the right people – using the right methods

Know your customers: identifying intelligence requirements

Who are your customers for competitor intelligence?

Your internal customers may broadly be divided into three main segments:

- senior managers
- middle managers
- tactical (i.e. sales, technical support, etc.).

Each of these segments will have their own individual competitor intelligence requirements. The range of requirements can put considerable pressure on a competitor intelligence operation and lead to it being pulled in various directions at the same time. To relieve the pressure on the competitor intelligence operation, customers should be graded for their relative importance. Here is a useful notation:

A   Hot customers – first priority
B   Warm customers – second priority
C   Cold customers – third priority.

Classifying customers A, B, or C is vital for the success of the competitor intelligence operation, particularly at the outset. Trying to satisfy too many customers too soon will undermine an otherwise well run operation.

The most important 'A' customers are likely to be senior managers, each of which should be treated as segments of their own. It is useful to gather background data on them in order to enhance your understanding of the drivers affecting their competitor intelligence requirements. Useful background data would include:

- existing intelligence wants/needs
- management style
- objectives
- drivers.

Why do they want or need competitor intelligence?

'It's important to decide the objectives of collecting competitor intelligence before you start collecting the data. Don't start collecting data until you've got a fairly clear idea of what you're going to use it for.'
Competitor intelligence analyst, BP

Radar/awareness intelligence or target intelligence?

It is absolutely crucial that a competitor intelligence operation manager understands the reasons why competitor intelligence is required. As we saw in the previous chapter, the two main types of competitor intelligence are radar/awareness intelligence and target intelligence. Intelligence products, such as news gathering and analysis, are produced on a continuous basis to improve awareness. Reactive in nature, they seek to answer the following questions:

RADAR/AWARENESS INTELLIGENCE
- Regular collection
- Standard requirements
- 'Panning for gold'

- What is going on out there?
- Is the change important?
- What are the implications of the change for our business?
- What should we do about it?

Information is sucked into the competitor intelligence operation and the competitor intelligence manager must determine the meaning, relevance and importance of particular pieces of information.

In contrast, target intelligence products are specific products commissioned to support the pursuit of specific business objectives or strategies. Target intelligence is trying to answer the question: What do I need to know to support this particular decision/strategy? Target intelligence can be used either for offensive purposes or for defensive purposes.

In target intelligence business objectives drive business strategies, which in turn determine the intelligence requirements; and these drive the information which is collected and the processes which are employed to handle, analyse and disseminate the intelligence produced.

TARGET INTELLIGENCE

- **Focused on specific strategies**
- **Specific intelligence requirements**
- **Likely to be one-off projects**

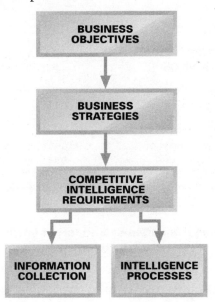

Fig. 3.1 Drivers of target competitor intelligence

Target intelligence is therefore objective led and is based on a need to know how to achieve objectives, while radar awareness intelligence is largely environment led. The latter is a 'panning for gold' exercise. It is an awareness exercise looking for opportunities and threats in the external environment from which to benefit, or against which the business needs to defend itself.

The distinction between radar awareness and target intelligence operations should not be taken too far. Ongoing monitoring of the environment is likely to need a list of 'need to knows', which is going to be influenced by the company's current or future business

strategies and objectives and target intelligence, which is by definition a focused exercise, which is going to need radar/awareness intelligence to help set specific pieces of raw information in context or to
improve our ability to make sense of the information.

In practice, a company's competitor intelligence operations are
normally a mixture of both types because each type of intelligence
has its own advantages and disadvantages. (*See* Figure 3.2.)

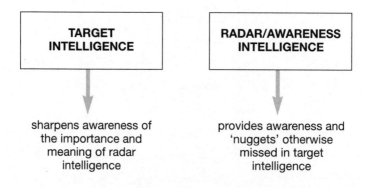

**Fig. 3.2 Radar/awareness and target intelligence are
mutually beneficial**

Relative benefits of radar/awareness and target intelligence

A good deal of the time the greatest benefits of competitor intelligence will frequently arise when it is produced in support of the
accomplishment of particular business strategies. Indeed, it is crucial
that as business objectives drive business strategies, these should in
turn drive intelligence requirements which themselves should determine both the information which is collected and the processes by
which the information is organised, analysed and disseminated.

It is true that in many companies business strategies are in a state
of permanent flux, which makes assessing intelligence requirements
all the more difficult. However, that is something every competitive
intelligence operation has to cope with.

CASE ILLUSTRATION

ABC is a manufacturing company in an increasingly competitive environment. It has set itself ambitious growth targets which it aims to achieve largely by acquisition. In the process it will be reducing competition, though this is not the primary objective. Identifying targets which fit the company's product profile is crucial. Collecting information on products and manufacturing capability is therefore high on the 'need to know' list.

Despite the obvious advantages of target intelligence operations, there is, however, always a need for radar/awareness competitor intelligence. Intelligence collected to support existing or planned strategies ignores current and potential threats and opportunities unconnected with these strategies.

To illustrate this point, it is helpful to think of the external information environment surrounding a business as made up of six segments. (*See* Figure 3.3.)

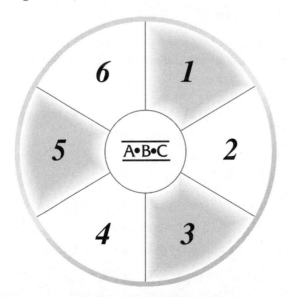

Fig. 3.3 Target intelligence has focus but can miss important developments

Three of these segments (1, 3, 5) are receiving the attention of the competitor intelligence manager because they concern particular issues of importance to internal intelligence customers. But the other segments (2, 4, 6) remain untouched by this attention. Threats and opportunities emerging from these segments are unlikely to be picked up by the intelligence-producing exercise associated with radar/awareness target intelligence operation.

'Great intelligence collection capability. Pity about the targeting.'

The invasion of South Korea by the North Koreans in 1950 was not predicted by the US intelligence community, despite their enormous intelligence-gathering capability. Part of the problem lay in the fact that monitoring North Korea's communications was not a priority. The intelligence failure was caused by poor targeting.

What competitor intelligence do your customers require?

This question should be broken down into the following component parts:

ASSESSING CUSTOMER REQUIREMENTS
- Who?
- Why?
- What?
- When?
- How?

- Customers' wants and needs. Is there a difference?
- Are their requirements strategic or tactical?
- Do they require information or intelligence?
- What are the target companies on which information is to be collected?
- What key intelligence requirements are to be collected on those target companies?

Each of these questions is considered below.

Wants or needs?

'You need to be an interpreter of wants into needs.'
Competitor intelligence manager

The distinction between wants and needs is an important one. Articulated wants are rarely the full picture of, say, a senior manager's requirements. They merely reflect what managers think they require. A competitor intelligence manager, while focusing on a customer's wants, must also see beyond wants to unexpressed needs, however difficult that may be. This can only be done by establishing good personal relationships with an internal customer, by researching and analysing the 'intelligence drivers' of the customer and by understanding the business. Intelligence drivers are those elements of the competitive environment which affect how well that manager performs and whether or not they will achieve their objectives.

Strategic or tactical requirements?

Strategic intelligence requirements generally refer to the broader and more long-term requirements of senior managers, while tactical requirements concern narrower and short-term issues, such as a salesperson's requirements for an individual competitor's prices.

There is not, of course, a precise distinction between strategic and tactical requirements, so there is a degree of arbitrariness in the classification below.

Strategic requirements
- new product development
- acquisitions and targets
- financial performance
- senior personnel charges

- joint ventures, alliances and offset deals
- opening up of new facilities or relocation of existing ones
- new launches.

Tactical requirements

- competitor prices
- competitor wins and losses
- key customers
- target customers
- marketing and sales tactics
- customer service and satisfaction.

Information or intelligence?

Within every company there is a requirement for competitor *information* as well as for competitor *intelligence*. Frequently managers use the word 'intelligence' indiscriminately without realising that there is a difference between the two concepts of intelligence and information. Although the difference between information and intelligence is not entirely clear-cut, *one useful approach is to consider intelligence as information which has been processed and analysed. A kind of 'added-value information'. (See Figure 3.4.)*

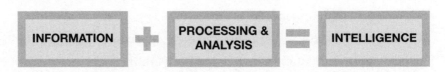

Fig. 3.4 The difference between information and intelligence

That is not to say that only intelligence is valuable. Individual pieces of information can be of enormous importance (for example, the news of a new product or service), though such pieces of information still require validation and therefore technically become intelligence before they can be used.

Senior managers frequently want both information and intelligence. They want news as well as analysis. This distinction is very important from the point of view of a competitor intelligence operation manager, because producing information can require a different kind of collection plan and a different set of processes to those required by intelligence. A demand for competitor information can be more easily satisfied by external open sources than can a demand for competitor intelligence.

Producing competitor intelligence involves more analysis than producing competitor information. Since analysis takes time, *intelligence production is normally a more time-consuming exercise than information production*.

Competitor, competitive or total intelligence?

While the focus of this book is on competi**tor** intelligence, it is important to realise that competitor intelligence is only one part of 'total' environmental intelligence. Many competitor intelligence managers are also analysing markets as well as competitors, and some are even charged with analysing the wider STEPP factors:

- Sociological
- Technological
- Economic
- Political
- Physical Environmental.

Monitoring the STEPP factors to identify future opportunities and threats can be very important. Technological change is there to be harnessed for competitive advantage. Competitors may be quicker than you in capturing a new technology and use that capture to attack your business.

Who are the target companies?

Identifying which companies to target for information collection is an important decision. Apart from the significance of choosing the right targets rather than the wrong targets, there are resource implications arising from the choice of targets. There are never enough resources to monitor all current and potential competitors. Selection is necessary, but, while it will reduce cost, selection will also increase the risk of missing important targets. *Balancing risk and cost is a vital but a difficult task.*

The range of possible targets which can be monitored is very wide. Apart from competitors – current, recent entrants and potential entrants – customers and suppliers, too, may be monitored for sales and marketing reasons or for the purposes of cost control. Non-competitors may be monitored in a non-competitive benchmarking exercise. Figure 3.5 illustrates the dilemma facing a business in terms of its intelligence 'focus'.

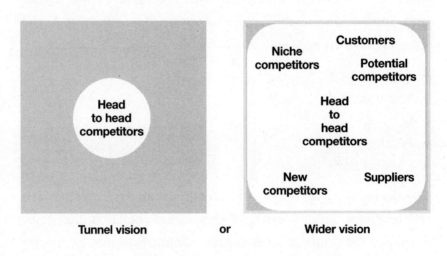

Fig. 3.5 Different views of the competitive environment

Among the potential target competitors from which you need to choose, there are a number of different types :

- head to head competitors
- niche competitors
- new competitors
- potential competitors.

In order to optimise expenditure, targets should be classified A, B or C which determines the desirable depth of research and the desired frequency of update. 'A' targets are those which have the highest level of monitoring. 'B' targets require periodic monitoring, while 'C' targets are 'back burners' and need only very limited periodic monitoring. How an individual target company is classified will depend on a number of criteria:

- the size of threat or opportunity
- the capability of competitor
- the probability of entry (for potential competitors).

What are the key intelligence requirements?

Key intelligence requirements (KIRs) refer to those aspects of a target about which information is to be collected. The list below indicates the sorts of competitor areas which may be of interest:

- relationships (e.g. alliances)
- driving forces (external and internal)
- objectives and intentions
- strategies and tactics (e.g. How they compete? Customer strategy, etc.)
- products and services (including prices)
- focus and targets
- methods and processes

- resources (e.g. people)
- performance
- strengths and weaknesses.

This structure will be examined in more detail in Chapter 6 which examines methods of analysing competitors.

The key intelligence requirements will vary from target to target and from customer to customer. Here are some of the requirements of some typical customers of the competitor intelligence operation. These are included as an illustration – not as a prescription for your own operation.

Sales

- sales arguments, tools
- strengths and weaknesses of competitors
- prices, discounts.

Business development

- strategies
- alliances or joint ventures
- business opportunities.

Product managers

- competitor product analysis
- strengths and weaknesses of products and services.

Strategic planning

- objectives and strategies
- alliances and joint ventures
- positioning.

Benchmarking

'The prime objective of benchmarking is to understand those practices that will provide competitive advantage in the marketplace.'
Paul Allaire, Chief Executive Officer for Xerox

The term 'benchmarking' is used to denote two different kinds of activities:

- comparing one company with another in terms of some aspect of their activities. For example:
  - plans
  - processes
  - performance
- gathering good ideas.

Companies benchmark against other companies either to identify objective standards against which their activities can be compared or to discover better ways to do something. Frequently the first leads to the second.

In terms of the choice of companies against which you should benchmark, there are three options:

- internal benchmarking
- external competitor benchmarking
- external non-competitor benchmarking.

For example, internal benchmarking consists of one part of, say, a global company comparing its activities against another part of the same company or gathering ideas to improve the way something is done. External competitor benchmarking is carried out to determine relative performance in key areas (e.g. market share) or to understand how a competitor does something – for instance, how it organises its salesforce.

Finally, non-competitive benchmarking is carried out less to determine competitive benchmarks (measures of comparison) than to discover improved ways of doing something which are common to your company and the non-competitor.

CASE ILLUSTRATION

The chairman of a UK company which sells widgets by mail order, and which was the number one in the marketplace, said that he was not interested in trends in his own industry. Instead, he was interested in mail order trends outside his own industry selling quite different products to quite different sets of customers.

The key questions you are trying to answer in competitor benchmarking are:

- Are we doing better than our key competitors in areas that matter?
- Are there any methods, processes and procedures employed by our competitors which we should adopt ourselves?

In non-competitive benchmarking the focus is on getting new, good ideas, which means that the key question is:

- Would profitability or competitiveness be improved by adopting superior practices?

This is where the phrase 'adopting best-in-class practices' can be so dangerous and misleading because the phrase can be both intimidating to managers of second-class operations and enticing because human nature wants to be best.

Businesses are not human beings. They need to be both profitable and competitive on an ongoing basis. Adopting 'best-in-class solutions' may be desirable to beat the competition and to maintain or increase profitability, but in contrast it may mean over-engineered so-called solutions with the costs of adopting the 'solutions' being greater than the benefits.

So how best to carry out competitive benchmarking? The key steps are set out below:

- Identify areas of importance.
- Select key variables and measures.
- Select appropriate companies with which to make comparisons.
- Measure own performance.
- Collect competitor information and evaluate.
- Identify relative strengths and weaknesses.
- Decide which relative weaknesses to improve.
- Implement change and measure results.

Among the most important steps are the selection of key areas to compare and the companies for comparison – the 'what?' and the 'who?' – which are, of course, the fundamental questions for any kind of competitor intelligence activity. In fact, competitor benchmarking and competitor intelligence are the same wine from two bottles with different labels. Non-competitive benchmarking can be useful, but has to be carried out with care if money is not to be wasted on the pursuit of over-the-top solutions.

CASE ILLUSTRATION

JCB benchmarks for competitiveness

There is a story told about Joe Bamford – the man who started JCB, the UK company which produces earth-moving equipment. He wanted to find out exactly what kind of excavator to produce and to find out he visited one building site after another around Britain. At each one he questioned the excavator drivers to find out what they disliked and what they really wanted.

What Joe Bamford was doing was benchmarking, though at that time the word had not been coined. However, he may not have known the word but he certainly knew how important benchmarking was for a company to succeed in a competitive environment.

Today at JCB, his example is followed as vigorously as ever. Among those primarily involved in benchmarking at JCB is the marketing team working for JCB-SCM Ltd, a joint venture with Sumitomo, based in Uttoxeter. The team consists of three managers: Mike Birks, Andrew Hornsby and Henry Warzybok. Their products include a range of 360° excavators.

Their philosophy towards the importance of benchmarking is clear. 'How do you know how good you are if you don't make comparisons' one of them remarked. Active ongoing benchmarking comes naturally to them. They are very much a 'hands on' marketing group. They are close to the customers, very competitive ('We like to come first') and have a major say in product development and re-development.

They spend a good deal of their time sizing up the opposition, either against existing JCB machines or against future models. When it comes to testing pre-production models they ensure the machines go to companies with considerable experience of competitor models.

The managers are also heavily involved in assessing the static and dynamic performance of individual competitor products. They call these evaluations 'Dig-offs', and from these they produce detailed evaluations of competitors' products.

They prefer to do dig-offs themselves to keep them under their own control rather than leaving them to the engineers. And while some competitors are innovative in the products they produce, others emphasise other aspects, such as after-sales service. JCB benchmark these as well.

But a crucial part of benchmarking is to identify the really important factors with which to compare your product with the competitors. Like all good benchmarkers the managers start with the customer. Using specially commissioned research they isolate the key customer requirements of the crucial decision makers. And by monitoring customers over time they can identify emerging trends.

But they don't just rely on other people's research. Many of the target benchmarks are also obtained face to face with customers.

The second stage of JCB's benchmarking process is to convert customer requirements into individual 'machine attributes'. Requirements, such as reliability, safety, ease of operation and driver comfort, are analysed into many attributes such as ease of maintenance, ergonomics and safety aspects, visibility and noise levels. The third stage is to convert these machine attributes into a product definition which goes to the design engineers. By controlling the benchmarking exercise, they are able to give development engineers specific standards they must meet in order to beat the competition. And engineers at JCB are used to rising to the challenges passed to them from benchmarking studies.

The pay-off of benchmarking comes in sales. Higher standards of performance against competitors produce strong arguments for JCB salesmen: they can stress JCB strengths and if necessary point to the weaknesses of competitors' machines.

JCB is a classic example of a market-driven company prospering despite major competitive threats. The competitive ethos of the founder, Joe Bamford, is echoed today in JCB's highly focused marketing team. To them benchmarking is just a way of life and a means of beating the competition.

When and how do your customers require competitor intelligence?

Target intelligence usually has a set deadline for completion, while awareness intelligence is required on a continuing basis.

Getting the information or intelligence to users in a form in which they can assimilate it quickly is also important. The range of communication mechanisms which can be used include:

- face to face
- electronic
- paper
- video
- audio.

Getting the balance right between paper and electronic mechanisms can be tricky. Some senior managers, despite agreeing at board level to an IT drive towards a paperless office, still prefer competitor information in paper form. Others like a computer disk from which the briefing can be transferred to their portable computer.

Apart from managers' preferences a competitor intelligence operation manager must consider what is most effective. Often the most effective and useful communication mechanism is, of course, face to face. Sometimes an audio tape is the best way of getting time with a senior manager. If he or she does a considerable amount of travelling they can play the tape in their car.

CASE ILLUSTRATION

One of the first things an American president reads each morning is the daily intelligence brief. Over the years presidents have differed in the kind of brief they want. Johnson (1963–69) wanted only one page. Nixon (1969–74) wanted the material in his daily briefing divided into two parts: fact and comment. Carter (1977–81) preferred longer briefs, while Ronald Reagan (1981–89) preferred his intelligence on videos.

How to identify what customers require

Methodologies

Whether the general requirement is radar awareness or target intelligence, strategic or tactical information, the practical process of identifying customers' requirements is an absolutely crucial step in running a competitor intelligence operation. Yet all too often companies rush this stage in their eagerness to reap the promised benefits of competitor intelligence. To repeat, identifying competitor intelligence requirements is an absolutely crucial stage and must not be skimped.

One commonly employed 'quick and dirty' method which is to be avoided if possible is the 'wish list'. Senior managers do not always know what intelligence they need. (Some are not even convinced that they need it at all, such is their ignorance of the increasing requirement for good business intelligence.)

Some senior managers will list all sorts of requirements 'from the top of their head' simply to avoid looking ignorant or because what they are uttering sounds useful. Often they are too busy to give much time to thinking clearly. But beware! Follow a wish list unthinkingly and you could end up being criticised at a later stage for producing intelligence of little value.

Always ask yourself 'What intelligence would be of most value?' Competitor intelligence requirements can be related to specific business objectives or to key success factors, or they can be a product of a benchmarking exercise.

A useful technique is the 'if only' procedure. Ask managers to think back and identify situations where competitor intelligence was not available and as a result either the company was hit by an unexpected competitor threat or the company missed a competitive opportunity.

Finally, one way of concentrating the mind on the potential value of competitor information is to consider the impact of specific pieces of information on your bottom line. Some of the items this kind of value analysis can produce are set out in Table 3.1.

Table 3.1 Value analysis focuses the intelligence effort

Value to company	Key intelligence requirement
£1m	Marketing strategy New product development, new process investment Acquisition
£100,000	New market entry, acquisitions
£10,000	Costs, weaknesses in customer relations Price changes

Interviews

Interviews should be subtle probings using indirect questions rather than overtly structured sessions using direct questions. Open-ended questions should be used rather than closed questions. Repeat your questions to see how consistent and coherent the person you are interviewing actually is. But you should disguise this repetition. Avoid producing a huge wish list of intelligence requirements. Where possible, get interviewees or participants to prioritise their perceived requirements.

Above all, you should focus as far as possible on the managers' own objectives, fears and hopes. Identify the decisions and issues they are facing and how intelligence can best add value to these decisions and issues. One way of questioning senior managers is to get them to identify the potential threats and opportunities which could affect the strategies they are responsible for implementing. If possible, try to get them to go further by identifying potential indicators of these threats and opportunities.

But a word of caution. Interviewing for competitor intelligence requirements is a delicate art. Remember most senior managers do not know what they really need and do not want to be reminded they do not know. Help them understand their needs. And do not expect to get all you need from the first interview. It is more important to build good relations.

Workshops

One good workshop is worth more than 20 interviews. It can produce more than interviews can ever provide – for instance, collective buy-in, joint focus and motivation.

However, planning a workshop is not a light task. But the fear of standing in front of an out-of-control or badly working workshop should motivate anyone! Successfully running a workshop (or any other group activity for competitor intelligence) is a matter of some important items and a host of small details.

Remember, 'perfection is a matter of trifles' and only by pursuing perfection will you achieve good standards on a bad day. The good days are just a bonus. Among the important items to consider when planning a workshop are:

- **Objectives**
  Be absolutely clear about what is the purpose of the workshop.
- **Hidden agendas**
  Identify the hidden objectives – usually concerned with specific people.
- **Number/Type**
  Think carefully about numbers and pattern of people.
- **Length**
  Half day? Full day? Two days?
- **Place**
  Avoid training areas near participants' offices. Get participants off-site if possible.
- **Style**
  Remember, a workshop is interactive and participative, not a lecture or a monologue.

● **Incentives**

These can work but it is very much a matter of 'horses for courses'.

● **Outputs**

Write up in blank forms the intended output of the workshop.

Interviews and workshops are useful in setting up a competitor intelligence operation. But requirements will change over time and must be constantly refined. (*See* Figure 3.6.)

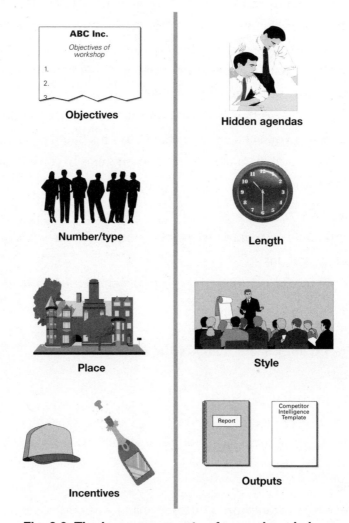

Fig. 3.6 The key components of a good workshop

Summary of Chapter 3

● Knowing your intelligence customers means identifying:
 – ho they are
 – why they require competitor intelligence
 – what competitor intelligence they require
 – when and how they require the competitor intelligence.

● It is important to prioritise customers and to avoid trying to please 'all the people all the time'.

● Intelligence requirements may be divided broadly into:
 – radar/awareness intelligence
 – target intelligence.

● Requirements should be analysed in terms of current and forecast wants and needs. Wants and needs are not the same.

● Competitor intelligence is likely to be only one component of the total intelligence requirements of a company.

● Competitive benchmarking aims to identify objective standards of competitive performance and also the processes which underpin this performance.

● Intelligence requirements may be obtained by:
 – background research
 – interviews
 – workshops
 – forecasts of business needs.

Troubleshooting

Common problems	How to deal with them
Supplying competitor intelligence for too many people	Prioritise your customers
'Tyranny of the telephone': never knowing what requests are coming next	Get behind the requests – get involved in decision making and forecast future requests
Many repetitive small requests taking lots of time	Systematise information on the 80:20 rule
Poor understanding of senior managers' requirements	Improve contact with, for instance, senior managers
Senior managers not seeming to use the information produced	Get feedback on intelligence provided
Poor interview and/or workshop skills	Develop or purchase relevant skills

Information collection

4

Constructing a collection plan

Internal sources
Human sources
Key success factors for internal networks
Ex-competitor staff

Competitor sources
Human sources
Hard copy sources
Electronic sources
Other competitor sources

Third-party sources
Human sources
Hard copy sources
Electronic sources: business databases
How to use business databases
Electronic sources: Internet
Electronic sources: media intelligence
Local intelligence sources

Airlines: two case illustrations
'The World's Favourite Airline'
Swissair's approach

Summary of Chapter 4

Troubleshooting

Constructing a collection plan

'There are two kinds of knowledge,
We know something,
Or we know where to find the knowledge.'
Dr Samuel Johnson

Once intelligence requirements are established and developed into agreed intelligence templates, the next task is to match these requirements with appropriate sources of information, a task which should be set out in a collection plan.

Constructing a collection plan involves carrying out a number of stages, which are illustrated in Figure 4.1.

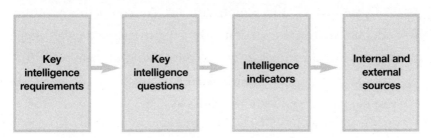

Fig. 4.1 From customer requirements to sources of competitor information

The procedure which should be carried out is as follows:

Step 1: Key intelligence requirements

Identify key intelligence requirements (KIRs) based on customer requirements.

Step 2: From KIRs to KIQs

Translate the KIRs into more specific key intelligence questions (KIQs). KIRs are frequently general in nature, for example: 'the current/forecast promotional methods of Competitor X to support product/service X in area B'. This general requirement needs to be turned into practical key intelligence questions, for example: 'What direct mail (or bill boards or press advertising) is Competitor X ...'.

Step 3: Identify indicators of change for KIQs

At this stage it may be possible for the key intelligence questions to be sourced directly. The KIQs may be fairly easy to collect and to identify sources for. For instance, a KIQ may be 'What is the competitor's financial performance for the last three years for which figures have been published?'. Because there are many sources which will give you this sort of information, you do not need to carry out indicator analysis.

If, however, the KIQ was 'When is the competitor going to relaunch product X?', this is more difficult. The competitor probably will not publish its relaunch. It may be a tightly guarded secret. Some third-party human sources, such as advertising agencies, printers, etc., may know the secret but may refuse to talk. In this case you will have to fall back on an indicator analysis.

What is an 'indicator analysis'? It is based on the observation that future corporate action (even if it is kept secret) is preceded by a pattern of pre-event signals. For instance, a relaunch may be preceded by the purchase of advertising space, the running down of old stock or the briefing of the salesforce. Identifying the pattern of indicators which precedes a particular action and the collection of information regarding those indicators constitutes indicator analysis.

Step 4: Identify potentially useful sources

We now need to identify those sources which are likely to be fruitful in answering the KIQs directly or in providing information on indicators. Such identification requires a clear classification of sources of competitor information. Here is the one developed at EMP, in which the sources of competitor information are divided into 'channel' types:

- internal sources
  - information inside your own company
- external sources
  - competitor sources
  - third-party sources.

Within each of these channel types of source information may be found various source types:

- human (or 'head' intelligence)
- hard copy material
- electronic files
- other.

Competitor information may therefore be found in any one of 12 possible source types. You need to build an intelligence collection grid for each KIQ. The grid for collecting information on a competitor's strategies will be quite different to one concerned with identifying sources of information on new product launches. An intelligence collection grid is illustrated in Figure 4.2.

Sources	Internal	External	
		Competitor	Third-party
Human			
Hard copy			
Electronic			
Other			

Fig. 4.2 Intelligence collection grid

Let us look at an illustration of the procedure for building up a collection plan. Let us say your key intelligence requirement is new product launches by a competitor (*Step 1*). This KIR is broken down into a number of key intelligence questions (*Step 2*), one of which is:

Is Competitor X going to launch a new product?

Brainstorming identifies a number of indicators of a new launch (*Step 3*), among which are:

- Recruitment
- Market research activity
- Buying media space.

The next step is to identify possible external sources of competitor information which are likely to have information on these three indicators (*Step 4*):

Indicator	External sources
1 Recruitment	Recruitment agencies
	Advertisements
	Headhunter activity
2 Market research activity	Pilot schemes
	Test marketing
3 Buying media space	Ad/PR agency
	Media buying agencies
	Printers

One of the purposes of the rest of this chapter is to give a broad picture of these different kinds of sources. This will enable you to choose the pattern of sources which, given the KIQs and indicators you have identified, will be most appropriate in terms of quality, fruitfulness and cross-validation and also in terms of accessibility, given the time available for collection.

An inappropriate pattern of sources or the overuse of one type of source has obvious implications for the quality of the final intelligence picture you are trying to construct. Sometimes the sheer number of sources of competitor information can be bewildering, which can force a person faced with tight deadlines to use the simple, easy-to-tap sources, such as electronic database information from third-party information providers. Be careful when you are doing that.

Internal sources

Human sources

A competitor intelligence system is only as good as the quality of information collected, and the most important sources of information are often internal sources. A competitor intelligence manager must create an internal network and energise the people in it to release the information inside their heads. Let no-one be misled: this is a mighty task, for there are none so difficult to move and motivate as your own colleagues! How much easier it is to use a computer information system, such as Reuters or Dialog or tap into the Internet.

Within your company there are many potentially fruitful human sources. The salesforce, of course, are considered to be of primary importance as an internal source of competitor information, and indeed they are, but there are other internal sources that can also be of considerable help. Any member of staff who has frequent contacts with significant customers, competitors or third parties picks up potentially useful information – for example, telesales or technical support.

Building an internal network means you have got to keep at it. You are like a salesperson who has to keep in contact with past and potential customers if the orders are going to keep flowing. So pick up that phone!

An internal network can be thought of as going through four stages in its development:

Stage 1: Start-up

At the beginning it is vital to create awareness of the competitor intelligence operation, its functions, its responsibilities and its staff. This awareness can be created by reports, entries in staff magazines and by personal contacts. It should also be created by selling competitor intelligence in the company and getting buy-in from important 'opinion-formers'.

Stage 2: Initial network

With the competitor intelligence operation off the ground, it is important to begin to identify important internal sources. This is done through contacts.

Stage 3: Build relationships

Having identified key potential sources (e.g. in advertising, sales and market research), see if you can provide any service for them to encourage their co-operation. In addition, identify key meetings and ensure you are included.

Stage 4: Fine tuning

As requirements change, the network will change. It is vital that the network evolves with the needs of the customers.

Key success factors for internal networks

As we have seen, building a network inside your company is one of the biggest and most important jobs you face. The following are the key success factors:

- budget
- understanding your organisation
- cultivating good personal relations

- persuasion plans
- motivation
- making the process of communication easy
- protecting your sources
- persistence
- focus.

Budget

Building up and running an internal network costs money. You need funds to establish good face-to-face relationships and money to top up that relationship and that may mean the resources to buy drinks or a meal. Not in any sense to bribe the contacts but merely to help to create and maintain the right relationship. Embassies understand this, so should commercial operations. Subject to cultural acceptance and senior manager support, money will also be needed to provide occasional incentives. Do not penny-pinch the internal network while throwing huge sums at database information or data filters.

Understand your organisation

This is an important requirement. You should know not only the formal organisation as revealed by organisation charts but also the unofficial one, the structure and frequency of meetings, and the positions and responsibilities of key players.

Cultivate personal relations

The best way of starting and maintaining a network is by personal contact. Even if distance and different time zones make this difficult and expensive, always aim to use personal contact at the beginning and 'top-up' the relationship from time to time.

Remember, it is a human network and personal relations are vital. Work hard to build relationships by Competitor Intelligence by

Walking Around (CIBWA)! Make contacts. Go to meetings. Build trust.

If you are going to build a fruitful human network, it is not going to be entirely composed of the easy-to-get-on-with and the nice-to-meet. It will include the awkward, the arrogant, the boring and even the less than pleasant. Unless you genuinely like people – the good, the bad and the ugly – you will not build that network.

A network is full of bilateral relationships, which over time are going to wax and wane and perhaps wax again. There has to be a lot of give and take to keep things on an even keel.

Persuasion plans

If you are creating groups or teams to monitor competitors, do make the meetings interesting and varied. Here is a sample outline persuasion plan:

Objective: Overcome resistance and gain the hearts and minds (and self-interest too) of key players.

Targets: (Say) Salesforce

Means:
1 Explain what information is wanted and why it is wanted.
2 Get their ownership of objectives.
3 Make the project *their* projects not just yours.
4 Ask – don't tell (or if you are telling them, disguise it).

Motivation

To keep the wheels of the network moving means you have to maintain interest and you must also consider incentives. If you are creating groups or teams to monitor competitors, make the meetings interesting and varied. Try team-building exercises at the beginning before you expect them to generate intelligence. Vary the style; use role playing, wargaming and simulations.

Consider incentives – both carrots and sticks

Convince senior managers that gathering or producing intelligence should be included in some managers' job descriptions. You can also use carrots but judiciously and appropriately: money for some, champagne for others depending on the culture of the company. Senior management recognition nearly always works. Demonstrate the added value contributed by competitor intelligence. It is vital to give credit, to praise. People need recognition. Acknowledgement of contributions is vital. In addition, you should provide feedback to those supplying you with information.

Make the process of communication easy

1 Ensure forms (hard copy or electronic) are simple and 'idiot-proof'
2 Always keep in touch by phone, voice mail and, if possible, personal contact.

Make the process of passing information to you easy and simple. Imagine it is five o'clock in the afternoon on a Friday and one of your internal network has just heard of a potentially important piece of information about a competitor.

You want that person to get that information to you as soon as possible. Yet think of the conflict of interests. What would make him or her delay going home after a hard week's work in order to contact you? What will matter is the invisible bond you have established between you. He or she is more likely to contact you if you have built up a good personal relationship in the past.

If the fax is the preferred channel of communication, produce fax pads which are simple to fill in. If the channel is voice mail, give them simple prompts to ensure the information is delivered in usable form.

In some cases you can encourage people to collect and transmit information by assigning responsibility to an individual or group of individuals for a particular competitor. That competitor becomes *their* competitor. But take care. If responsibility is given to the group, attention must be given to the dynamics of the group, otherwise it will ossify and fail in its mission.

Protect your sources

One crucial factor in encouraging information out of the minds of colleagues is to respect their confidence and protect them as sources. If you do not, your sources will dry up. This is particularly the case with senior internal sources and external human sources.

Persistence

Don't give up. 'Faint heart never won fair lady', and building up a successful competitor intelligence operation takes effort over a period of time. So the rule is: keep at it. You will have successes and failures, losses and gains, but keep on building and nurturing your network. One big compensation is that the better the network, and the more it rests on *your* shoulders, knowledge and expertise, the more indispensible you are making yourself.

Focus

As in most things, it is important to focus. Grade the people in your network according to their potential as sources. Allocate your time and effort in the direction of the perceived greatest return. Your time is valuable. Allocate it wisely.

Active senior champion

One final point. People will be more easily moved if there is an active senior champion. As previously mentioned, getting and *keeping* a senior champion is a key success factor.

Ex-competitor staff

Apart from building an internal human network of sources, you will also need to build into your management of internal sources the debriefing of ex-competitor staff who join your company. The extent to which these staff can help you will obviously vary according to the terms of their contract with their previous employer.

Debriefing them as they join the company must be done very carefully and at first casually so as to allay suspicions and enable you to judge character. Some managers, it is true, are more than willing than others to talk about their previous employment.

Others are more reticent and may be best approached by asking them for their assessment of the strengths and weaknesses of the current employer compared with the previous one. Seek their advice in interpreting specific pieces of information. Reassure them of their status as a confidential source, otherwise they may clam up.

Competitor sources

Human sources

These fall into two categories: current employees and ex-employees now working in your organisation. Current employees may be contacted directly but are frequently unlikely or unable to talk. Nevertheless, information can legitimately be gathered from three channels:

- conference presentations
- trade shows
- industry/technical meetings.

Conference presentations

Hundreds of conferences take place each year, some of which provide platforms for speakers from competitor companies. You should attend these conferences, not to present but as an opportunity for networking and information gathering. However, only so much time can be spared going to conferences, etc. The trick is to get other people to do the work for you.

Using trade shows

Trade shows are valuable sources of competitor intelligence. The main steps you need to take to extract good information from the trade shows are set out below:

- Construct a plan:
  - Identify objectives, key targets, KIRs and KIQs.
- Preparation:
  - Pre-register, collect information on targets.
  - Before you get to the show, do your homework on the people and organisations that are going to be present at the show.
- Build a competitor profile template:
  - Create a structure which identifies what information you seek and how it is going to be presented.
- Plan your visits to the stands:
  - Plan both the timing and number of visits.
- Ask the right questions:
  - Draft the key questions beforehand – but do not use notes when asking!
- Home in on the technical people:
  - They may be less difficult.
- Circulate results fast.

Industry/technical meetings

Most industries have some sort of regular meetings of representatives from competing companies. While limited in the scope they offer for competitor intelligence gathering, nevertheless they are useful for general awareness and for picking up industry gossip and speculation. Treat them seriously. Always write a brief list of main points picked up and make sure all contacts are listed in your files. It is extremely important to keep good records at all times.

Hard copy sources

Competitors leak information in the normal course of their business. Here are some of the more obvious examples:

- adverts – product and employment
- product and corporate brochures
- reports and accounts
- press releases and PR
- quotations
- patents
- Stock Exchange filings
- in-house magazines
- adverts for new staff
- Email, web, etc.

Obvious as it may seem, it is important that competitor hard copy information which is collected is both dated and correctly filed. To ensure up-to-dateness, an ongoing active collection of competitor hard copy production should take place.

Electronic sources

The primary competitor sources of electronic information are:

- websites
- video or audio tapes (i.e. radio and television).

The huge growth of websites in the last few years provides researchers with considerable opportunities to take advantage of the naivety of companies in loading their websites with far more information than they should. Radio and television can also contain information provided by companies.

Other competitor sources

Direct experience of a competitor's product or service can be achieved in a number of other ways:

- observation – going to see competitor's shop, offices, plant, hotel, aircraft, etc.
- purchase – fly the competitor's aircraft, buy a service contract, etc.
- 'tear down'/reverse engineering – buy and dismantle a product to evaluate its cost, profit and performance potential.

Third-party sources

Third-party sources are external sources which are not direct competitor sources, but which are indirect channels of information from competitors or about competitors.

Human sources

A wide variety of third-party human sources may have significant pieces of relevant information. Some may be customers of competitors, others may be business partners, or organisations employed by the competitors. Still others may collect information on competitors as part of their normal work, such as brokers, credit rating organisations and market research organisations.

A classification of third-party human sources follows:

Customers

This group may be divided into two main groups:

- current customers
- former customers.

To collect information from customers, a number of approaches can be taken such as:

- customer satisfaction surveys
- specifically targeted research (e.g. win/loss analysis).

Organisations working for or with the competitor

- business partners/joint ventures
- advertising agencies
- agents and distributors
- designers and printers
- PR firms.

Organisations selling to the competitor

- raw material suppliers
- IT suppliers.

Organisations monitoring the competitor

- brokers
- credit rating organisations.

Other human sources with a knowledge of the competitor

- academics (e.g. business schools)
- competitors of the competitor

- employment agencies
- government officials
- market researchers
- members of pressure or interest groups
- trade unionists
- journalists.

Even neighbours of the target company can be useful. Here is an example. Asked to monitor the activities of a UK company, a researcher called on the industrial neighbour of the target company and literally found an Aladdin's cave of information. It transpired that the target company had for several years been trying to get the neighbour to quit its premises so it could control the whole site. As a result this neighbour had been collecting enormous amounts of information on the target company. This information he was more than happy to share.

Hard copy sources

Hard copy information on competitors may be tapped via third-party sources from the following sources.

HARD COPY SOURCES
- Brokers' reports
- Ratio comparisons
- Market research reports
- Case studies
- Court cases
- Government publications
- Aerial photos
- Remote sensing
- Planning documents
- Land registry
- Libraries
- Cuttings agencies

- **General press** – useful for three types of work. First, as raw material for producing 'crash' analysis: quick assessments of new situations, companies or issues. Second, for identifying early 'leaks' of future action by competitors. Third, for picking up scattered nuggets for collation.

- **Brokers' publications** – these are most important sources. Often their reports contain information not otherwise available. A must for most research.

- **Business ratio publications** – useful for making financial bench-marks between companies.
- **Market research reports** – useful for market share information and they sometimes include useful, if summarised, information on other aspects of companies.
- **Case studies** – a very inexpensive source of generalised back-ground material on companies. Occasionally the case studies are of particular value because they are up to date and because of the depth of the research which has gone into them.
- **Court cases** – a useful source of information concerning the liti-gation entered into by the target company.
- **Official publications** (e.g. UK Monopolies and Mergers Commis-sion reports) – sometimes these reports contain useful material extracted from competitor companies, such as cost information.
- **Aerial photographs and remote sensing** – remote sensing con-sists of satellite imagery, ranging from photographic imagery to imagery used, for instance, to monitor crop yields.
- **Planning documents/environmental filings** – these can be very valuable for providing information on plant organisation and layout, and on extensions or other plant developments.
- **Land Registry documents** – useful in the UK for identifying the owner of sites and the length of leases.

A number of organisations are useful in bringing together a number of these hard copy sources:

- **Libraries – for instance in the UK**
  - City business library
  - business schools libraries
  - Science Reference Library.
- **Cuttings agencies** – only some local newspapers are available electronically either through commercial databases or via the Internet. Frequently the only convenient way of getting editorial

and advertisement copy from local newspapers is to obtain cuttings from a cuttings agency. The problem with cuttings is that after circulation they tend to be filed and forgotten. They do not permit easy retrospective searches for words, phrases or references that you *know* are there, but cannot find.

Electronic sources: business databases

There are hundreds of publicly available business information files which can be searched online from a computer via a modem and many are also available via CD-Rom. Access to the information is sold by a number of large host systems, such as the Dialog Corporation, FT Profile or Lexis Nexis. Sometimes a business information file is sold by more than one host system.

Some business information can be searched via a CD-Rom on one's own computer. While relatively expensive to buy, they are cheaper in the long run to use compared to online searching if many searches have to be made of the same data files. Filtered electronic information is also sold by companies such as Individual, ESMERC and Oxford Analytica. All filtered services are only as good as their coverage of the sources relevant to the inquiry.

Some business information files contain the text of newspapers, trade journals or brokers' reports. Others contain statistics, patents or trade marks.

Here are some important host systems:

- America Online
- Compuserve
- Data Times
- Dialog Corporation (Dialog, Datastar, MAID)
- Dow Jones
- FT Profile
- Lexis-Nexis

- News Net
- Reuters.

Identifying the best business information file and host can be achieved by using one or more of the following directories:

- *The Online Manual: A Practical Guide to Business Databases* (Learned Information)
- *The Instant Guide to Company Information Online – Europe* (British Library)
- *Full Text Sources Online* (Bibliodata)
- *The Prentice Hall Directory of Online Business Information*
- Mick O'Leary, *The Online 100* (Pemberton Press)
- *The Online Deskbook* (Pemberton Press).

Further details of the last two publications may be obtained from the following website: www.onlineinc.com/pempress. Other useful websites for keeping up to date are www.infotoday.com/catalog/direct.htm and www.infotoday.com/catalog/books.htm.

Some host systems have an index file to the files which allows you to identify which files are relevant to your keywords. Two examples are the CROS file in DataStar.

When selecting potentially useful business information files, you need to have in mind the following:

- How up-to-date do I need the information in the business information file to be?
- How complete a copy of an original (probably hard copy) publication do I require?
- Will abstracts be a satisfactory substitute for full text?

Let us assume you wish to tap business information files for a purpose that requires the information to be bang up-to-date, and that you wish to have complete coverage of the editorial sections of the publications covered and that you want full text.

By using a publication such as *Full Text Sources Online*, you can check the key journals and newspapers you wish to cover to discover whether the entries in the file are merely some of the articles in the publication or full editorial coverage. You can also contact the file producers for information on the lag between publication date and electronic input.

How to use business databases

One of the problems with business databases is that they can give a false sense of instant knowledge. Anyone who has typed in some keywords into a computer logged on to one of the host systems knows how beguiling they can be. Apparently relevant information is there at the touch of a button. It is all too easy to spend far too much time and money searching business databases. Some pointers to enable you to use them wisely are set out in Figure 4.3.

Step 1 Identify key intelligence requirements and develop into key intelligence questions

Step 2 Carry out a text analysis of relevant articles

Step 3 Identify useful databases

Step 4 Build draft thesaurus and test

Step 5 Use thesaurus to filter raw material

Fig. 4.3 How to 'pan for gold' in business databases

One of the problems of searching business information files in the English language is the imprecision with which journalists use words. Take the words *acquisition* and *divestment*. All kinds of other words apart from these are used by journalists, such as: *disinvestments, merger, bid, takeover, hostile bid, offer, disposals, deals, purchase, approaches, in talks with, acquiring sell operations*. Another example is the word 'litigation'. Tracking the litigation of a company requires the use of a variety of search words, such as: *trial, dispute, liability, damages, legal action, lawsuit, claim.*

For example, if we wish to monitor the changing strategies of Sainsbury, a leading food retailer in the UK, the search rule will be SAINSBURY + KEY WORD(S). But what key word(s)? Well, obviously the first keyword will be STRATEG*. The asterisk means the word is 'truncated' and the computer will pick up words such as STRATEGY, STRATEGIES and STRATEGIC. But when we analyse the results of this exercise, we find that STRATEG* brings in only about 45 per cent of the useful articles.

Another 25 per cent comes in articles which do not include variations of the word stem STRATEG* but instead include variations of the word stem PLAN*. This is to some extent predictable but most of the remaining 30 per cent of useful articles are picked up from using the word stem SCHEME*, which we did not expect. The reason why SCHEME* is so useful is because it has been used by journalists to describe the loyalty card SCHEMES, which, of course, is a very important customer loyalty strategy. Some journalists continued to use the word scheme to describe other strategies.

It may sound like heresy but if you want to be bang up-to-date about information in trade journals or if you want full coverage of all elements in a particular trade journal, then in many cases good 'ole fashioned hard copy may be the best for you. Why? For three main reasons:

- some information providers do not input the contents of a trade journal onto their files until days or even weeks after hard copy publication
- only a part of the hard copy publication is made available electronically.
- only some of the important journals may be covered by the database or filtered service.

The message is: horses for courses. For less urgent work, for quick updates (without always being right up to date) for getting an overview of a situation, then database services are very helpful. But if you want real-time information, use hard copy backed up with newswires and sometimes the Internet, which is somewhat strange in this age of the electronic super-highway!

And one last tip. Always insist that information providers or filtered information services produce a list of their sources *before* you commit much of your budget into their care. Use it to identify important gaps in their coverage. Get them also to reveal the lag between hard copy publication and availability on their systems, and also to identify how much of the publication is available on-line and whether entries are full text or abstracts.

Don't be beguiled by ease of searching or the easy availability of so-called 'filtered' information on your computers. Unless, of course, your internal intelligence customers do not mind you providing a partially out-of-date information service.

Electronic sources: Internet

All kinds of competitor information, some of which are not otherwise easily available (e.g. interest groups), can be obtained via the Internet. Much of it is free, though some commercial services, including those provided by the online hosts mentioned above, are introducing information-for-a-fee services, a trend which appears set to continue in the future.

The Internet can be useful for finding all kinds of information. The following is a very short summary of some of the competitor intelligence resources on the Internet.

● **Competitor information**
  - company websites
  - annual reports
  - filings
  - company adverts
  - trademarks and patents
  - trade shows.

● **Third-party information**
  - company profiles
  - brokers' reports
  - news
  - market and industry information
  - credit reports
  - stockmarket information
  - groups and industry experts
  - government and official information sources
  - scientific, technical and medical sources
  - country information.

Searching the Internet can either be achieved by locating a site for which one already has the site address, or by locating sites via a directory or search engine. The main general directory is Yahoo (www.yahoo.com). There are many search engines, so the following represents a very short summary:

● major search engines – Alta Vista, Lycos, Excite, Northern Light, Infoseek, Hotbot

- specialist search engines – Newsbot, Deja News
- regional search engines – Euroferret
- meta search engines – Ask Jeeves, MetaCrawler, Inference Find.

Searching the Internet may give you some unique information but great care must be taken to avoid wasting time. Build up a directory of useful websites so as to avoid using search engines (such as Alta Vista) unnecessarily.

Electronic sources: media intelligence

Radio and TV services can sometimes be very revealing. They are very up-to-date and give you the next best thing to direct contact with decision makers. A video of an interview with a senior manager of a competitor company is often of immense interest to his or her equivalents in your company. Videos in particular can be used to judge character by studying body language and even to predict strategies or tactics.

Local intelligence sources

Going to the location of the competitors' plant or office is often useful. Simply to replace a vague impression with concrete sensory information can help thinking. Local sources of information can often be far more informative than national newspapers or journals. Local newspapers (paid and free) cover such things as new capital expenditure, hirings and firings and the speeches of senior managers visiting the plant.

It is rarely possible in Britain to find all the intelligence you need from 'national' sources such as press or trade journals. And because few, if any, local newspapers in Britain are available online, and only some of them are clipped by the agencies, it is frequently necessary to visit a local library. Sometimes this takes you to one of the quaintly named towns – such as Chipping Sodbury or Ramsbottom.

There one can tap into the local newspapers, including the free newspapers which have sprung up all over Britain in the last 30 years. Although they are almost entirely vehicles for advertising, nevertheless they do attempt to maintain an image of still being a newspaper by including a few articles.

Sometimes these articles are entirely about a local company, and on occasions they are very valuable sources of intelligence. Frequently, they contain photographs of business operations, and on one occasion an article had a photograph of the company's entire production line. A copy of the photograph was purchased, enlarged and showed to an engineer who was then able to provide all sorts of valuable intelligence about the company's operations.

For some reason, heads of companies will open their mouths and their factories to local newspapers, something they would never dream of doing to a trade journal or a business newspaper such as the *Financial Times*.

Local libraries sometimes have cuttings files on the more significant local companies and, if you are fortunate to be able to get into the library of the local newspapers, their files are often extremely useful. Local governments keep files of planning applications which sometimes include such useful items as letters explaining the need for investment or full floor plans of the existing or proposed factory.

Environmental impact studies must be submitted with planning applications for industrial developments, and these will contain much valuable technological information about the proposed development.

In Britain the Land Registry is very useful for identifying the owner of the buildings and, if leased, the length of the lease.

Local universities and colleges sometimes have staff knowledgeable in local industry or services and occasionally will have produced or even published directories of local companies. These sometimes contain information not otherwise available.

Local intelligence

EMP Intelligence Service was once given the job of tracking a small subsidiary of a large holding company in one of the other countries of the European Community. The client had previously used conventional sources but all they had been given were the annual reports and accounts for the holding company. A check on the usual databases turned up relatively little information and indicated that we would have to 'go local'. An added factor was that the client wanted any information that was located translated into English.

Since the target company was in the fashion trade, it was decided to tap its advertisements both in print and on radio/television, as well as pick up copies of its brochures from a variety of third parties, some of which were also useful for intelligence on customer attitudes and on future developments. A list of newspapers and trade journals, general and specific, was obtained and matched up against the coverage of databases such as Textline and also of clippings agencies such as the London-based Romeike and Curtice. This analysis identified that the local newspaper in the target town was not covered by either of the information channels mentioned above.

This led to one of the great delights of competitive intelligence work – a visit to the town of the target, and a chance to savour – albeit briefly – the food of a different country. A visit to the local public library revealed back files of the local newspaper. It was not difficult to arrange a local researcher to scan the last year's output and provide translations, a task made easier by the existence of a card index to local news.

The articles the researcher translated proved remarkably revealing – amazingly so since there was little or no coverage of that firm's affairs in the national and trade press. Details of the company's test market activities were obtained and as a result it was decided to monitor the target's test marketing activities in the future. This was to give our client important advance warning of new products.

One surprise was the pile of literature which was collected by visiting the small public exhibition in the entrance area of the target company's plant. One leaflet which was picked up was aimed at the local population and contained details of the company's proposed expansion, the reasons for the expansion, together with all sorts of details about the company's future strategies!

Airlines: two case illustrations

Sixty years ago a crucial wartime battle had more or less come to an end in the North Atlantic. To most observers, it had apparently been a conflict between, on the one side, convoys of merchant ships and their protectors and, on the other, groups of submarines.

Yet in reality it was more a fight between two intelligence organisations back in Europe, each striving for superior knowledge of the other side's positions and intentions. It was their relative success or failure against each other that crucially determined the ultimate outcome of the deadly duel out in the Atlantic between the surface ships and their underwater foes.

Sixty years on, another Battle of the Atlantic is raging and still increasing – not, however, at sea but in the air. This time it is between the major international airlines. Already it has 'sunk' Pan Am, one of the oldest and most venerable of the international airlines. And in the last few years the battle has become increasingly competitive.

Faced with questions over their very survival, some airlines have turned increasingly, and not surprisingly, to competitor intelligence, which has today become a vital tool in their competitive management.

'The World's Favourite Airline'

One airline in particular has emerged to become one of the dominant players in international air travel: British Airways. From being the object of sick jokes only 20 years ago (BA? Stands for B****y Awful!), the airline has become the most profitable major international airline in the world, and one which is highly respected – even feared – by other airlines.

Part of their success was undoubtedly due to the clear determined leadership of BA's former Chief Executive Officer, Lord King, brought in by the then Prime Minister Margaret Thatcher to revive the inefficient and unprofitable state airline and to privatise it. But part of the success has also been due to British Airways' use of competitor intelligence (not, of course, British Airways' use of illegal espionage methods against Virgin Airways, which hit the headlines in the early 1990s).

British Airways' drive for competitive advantage

In the early 1990s British Airways adopted seven corporate goals:

- global leadership
- good financial performance
- service and value
- customer performance
- safety
- good employer
- good neighbour.

British Airways measured its own performance and then benchmarked that performance against the performance of selected target competitors. British Airways chose six international airlines as targets, two each from the United States, Europe and the Far East:

- Lufthansa

- Swissair
- Delta
- United
- All Nippon
- Singapore.

The unit in British Airways that was charged with the responsibility of benchmarking other airlines was a department within BA's Corporate Strategy Department called 'Market Place Performance' based near Heathrow Airport to the west of London.

At one time the unit had a staff of six, two of whom at any moment were travelling on competitor airlines. The unit used benchmarking to:

- identify deviations from benchmarks
- flag significant problems
- eliminate failpoints
- aim for zero defects.

Swissair's approach

British Airways is not the only European airline to use competitor intelligence to enhance its competitive performance. One of its own benchmark targets – Swissair – also has a competitor intelligence unit.

Swissair have used competitor intelligence to enable the airline to remain competitive and to assist it in making bold tactical moves against its competitors. It regularly collects intelligence on its competitors – for instance, on Lufthansa – in a number of ways.

The competitor intelligence department of Swissair is located in Zurich. It receives information largely from internal services and third-party sources. Figure 4.5 sets out the main flows into the organisation.

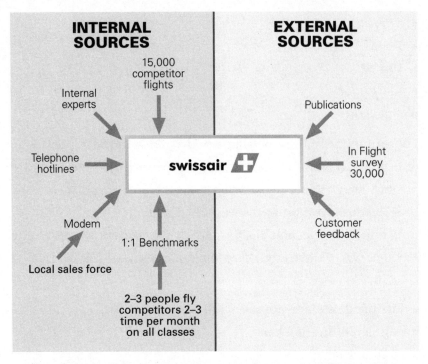

Fig. 4.4 Sources of competitor information used by Swissair

Internal sources

Like British Airways, Swissair collects competitor intelligence through members of the competitor intelligence unit travelling on competitors' airlines. They, too, have two staff travelling on competitor airlines carrying out checks on a variety of aspects of competitors' performance, ranging from the size and colour of trays and the layout and type of food to the organisation of the galley.

Swissair's competitor intelligence department also obtains information from their salesforce in other countries by means of an online link between headquarters and sales office. Communication is via a modem.

Staff are also encouraged to communicate information to the unit by means of a telephone and fax. Special numbers are allocated for this purpose. The unit also draws information about competitors from other departments within Swissair.

Finally, a major source of information about competitors comes from the 15,000 flights a year which Swissair staff make on competitor airlines. Travellers on competitor airlines were asked to analyse a host of details. Some examples are shown in Figure 4.5.

A special machine-readable form has been devised to facilitate the process of recording the information and also in producing monthly assessments.

External sources

Swissair's competitor intelligence unit uses three main sources of external intelligence. First are publications which are used to cross-check information coming in from other sources. The other sources use customers for information. Around 30,000 useable in-flight questionnaires are analysed and fed into the intelligence system. Finally, there is feedback from individual customers.

Competitor intelligence in support of a major tactical competitive move

Competitor intelligence has also been used by Swissair in planning a tactical strike against its competitors.

In the early 1990s Swissair faced a problem. It was being hit by a decline in the number of business passengers flying with Swissair who chose to fly business class. Over two years the percentage of business passengers flying economy increased by 15 per cent.

On investigation Swissair identified that business passengers saw little difference between business class and economy class. But Swissair identified a wider problem: that between airlines there was little brand loyalty. Load capacity was being determined more by timetable and price.

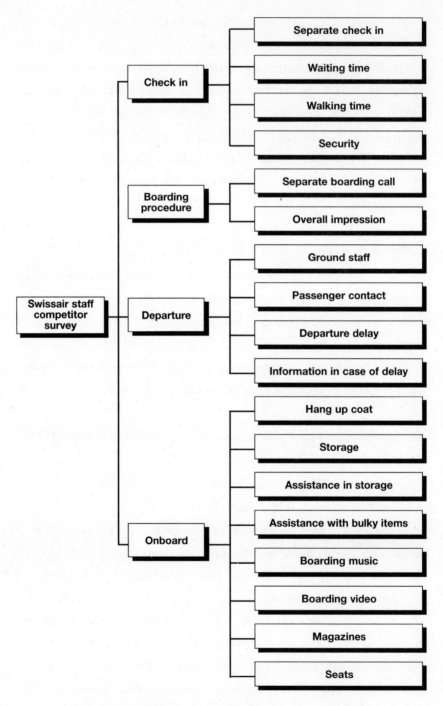

Fig. 4.5 Swissair's key intelligence requirements

As a result, to combat falling revenues, Swissair decided in 1992 to differentiate their business class both against competitors and against economy class in a number of ways:

- reduction in the number of seats across the plane from 2 + 3 to 2 + 2
- increased seat width
- changed design of trays
- priority baggage.

Summary of Chapter 4

- Sources divide into three channel types:
    - internal sources (inside the organisation)
        - external sources – competitor
        - external sources – third party.
- Each channel type subdivides into four source types:
    - human ('head') intelligence
    - hard copy
    - electronic
    - other (e.g. TV and radio).
- For both internal and external sources, a collection plan should be constructed which contains the following steps:
    - identification of key intelligence requirements (KIRs)
    - KIRs are broken down into key intelligence questions (KIQs)
    - KIQs are analysed into indicators
    - relevant sources are identified.
- The key success factors for building a successful internal human intelligence network are:
    - budget
    - knowledge of organisation
    - persuasion plans

- cultivation of personal relations
- motivation
- convenient communication process
- protection of sources.

● Competitor sources include:
- human sources: conferences, trade shows and meetings
- hard copy: brochures
- electronic: websites, radio and television.

● Third-party sources include:
- human sources: customers, suppliers, etc.
- hard copy: brokers' publications, reports, etc.
- electronic: databases, websites, etc.

● Business databases and data filter services should be evaluated by the following criteria:
- source coverage
- degree of hard copy selection
- abstracts or full text
- lag between hard copy publication and electronic entry.

● The Internet is an increasingly valuable source but requires expertise to avoid considerable wastage of time.

● Local intelligence may be very revealing, using such sources as:
- local people
- local newspapers, planning documents, land registry documents, etc.
- local organisations (e.g. newspapers, colleges).

Troubleshooting

Common problems	How to deal with them
Inappropriate balance of sources, given intelligence requirements	Build a coherent collection plan
Little information is received from internal sources	Build an internal network of sources
Lack of personal skills to develop internal network	Acquire skills or change personnel
Poor/inadequate organisation skills	Acquire skills
Ignorance of sources	Acquire knowledge
Electronic information overwhelms the competitor intelligence operation	Revisit collection plan and/or negotiate additional resources

5

Analysing competitors

From information to intelligence

First stage: Analysis

Pre-collection source selection/filtering
Evaluation
Indexing, filing and collation
Synthesis/Description
Forecasting/Speculation

Second stage: Analysis

Competitive opportunities and threats
Competitive strengths and weaknesses analysis
Competitive and business environment analysis
Competitor modelling/value chain
Key success factor (KSF) analysis
Market position analysis

Summary of Chapter 5

Troubleshooting

From information to intelligence

'Quantity derives from measurement
Figures from quantities
Comparisons from figures
And victories from comparisons.'
Sun Tzu

The word analysis is a big word. It adds weight to statements, and for that reason it tends to be over-used. Sometimes, the word analysis is used to describe the entire range of processes of collation/synthesis, forecasting and making assumptions. More usually, it is used to describe the specific mental processes associated with the following:

- making sense of a number of pieces of raw information
- assessing their importance or significance
- the exercise of brain or intuition which produces new insights
- a process of adding meaning.

In some cases analysis will involve making comparisons; in others, it consists of breaking down raw information into component parts in order to shed light on the underlying factors; while in others, it will involve building up a composite picture from individual pieces of raw or partially processed information. There are eight steps through which a piece of raw information may pass, as Figure 5.1 illustrates.

Steps 1–6 are examined in the rest of this chapter. Steps 7 and 8 will be examined in Chapter 6.

First stage: Analysis

Pre-collection source selection/filtering

The first stages in producing intelligence – identifying requirements and the sources which need to be tapped are themselves analytical

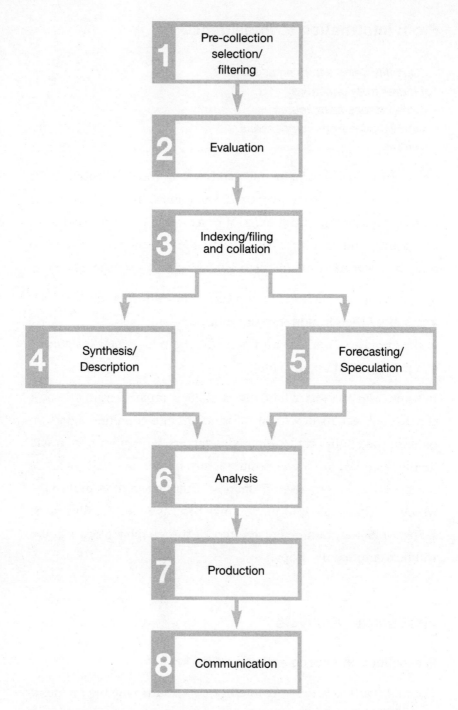

Fig. 5.1 From raw information to the communication of intelligence

processes. Because the quality of whatever output is produced depends ultimately on how well the first steps are carried out. You cannot build good intelligence on poor requirements and poor information.

Evaluation

Some of the information we collect is obtained by direct sense experience (e.g. a plant visit) but frequently most of the raw information we have about a target comes to us via indirect mechanisms. As a consequence, information about important key intelligence requirements/questions usually needs some form of evaluation. It cannot just be assumed to be accurate, for instance, just because it is published in the *Financial Times*, and, by the same token, rumours are not necessarily inaccurate. But not all articles in the press can be checked, though obviously not all unchecked competitor information will be of the same quality as an article in the *Financial Times*.

Evaluating raw competitive information is always a vital step in the intelligence process. Most of the intelligence failures in history – national, military and commercial – have not been failures in collection but failures of organisation or evaluation, which is why epistemological concerns are so important.

Epistemology is the philosophy of how we know what we know. And it takes but a moment of thought to realise that epistemology must of necessity be at the heart of our work. For the collection and analysis of information about the competitive environment must involve a careful appreciation of how we go about knowing, and must include an equally careful assessment of what we do know and also *what we do not know*.

A crucial part of the indexing procedure is the evaluation given to a particular piece of raw material. While much of externally produced information 'arrives' with date and source included, not so internal information. For this kind of information the following classification has been found to be useful:

- checked fact
- assumed fact
- published material
- rumour.

Rumours are important. They can be early signals of future change. Most senior managers are only too glad to receive rumours – as long as they know they are just rumours and what their source is. But not all senior managers are like-minded. As Voltaire put it: 'There are men who can think no deeper than a fact'.

Some writers designate information as either hard or soft. They consider, for instance, 'facts, statistics and quantitative information' to be hard information. This appears rather optimistic and unrealistic. A good deal of statistics and quantitative information are little better than published information or assumed facts. In many cases, statistics and quantitative information are unlikely ever to be classified as checked fact simply because much quantitative data is simply uncheckable.

So-called 'soft information' is considered by some to include opinion, commentary, conjectural/musings, anecdotal evidence and rumours. Opinions and commentaries are better classified as assumed facts or published material while the latter three are subsets of rumour. As was observed earlier it is best not to use the hard/soft classification at all. (You will find additional treatment of the hard-soft classification on pages 33–4).

Indexing, filing and collation

The purpose of indexing is not merely to enable raw information to be retrieved at a later date, but to permit pattern analysis to be performed on the information, and to facilitate the management of sources. Pattern analysis is made possible by appropriate indexing of raw information, so that raw information may then be manipulated into a variety of lists.

These lists may be arranged in a variety of ways – for instance, by subject, source, form of analysis, or by date and evaluation. Some examples are given below:

- **Subject**
  - competitor
  - country/geographical area
  - market
  - product.
- **Source**
  - evaluation
  - type of source.
- **Form of analysis**
  - opportunity and threat
  - strength and weakness
  - importance.
- **Time**
  - date of publication
  - date of collection.

Filing is a fundamentally important subject, but is little regarded and so often ignored or not given the attention that it deserves. Unfortunately, this attitude is a threat to an efficient intelligence system. All systems of competitor intelligence must have efficient and effective filing systems, for both hard copy information and for electronic information.

Hard copy filing

A good system of storage and retrieval for competitor intelligence *must* contain a good hard copy system. Not all competitor information will arrive in electronic form or can easily or cost effectively be scanned in electronically. Yet all too often, little thought is given to the type of manual filing system. Filing is, presumably, not the most attractive of activities. Yet you ignore the problem of manual filing at your peril – unless of course you have the resources to scan everything into a computer electronically (or send it to Indonesia for double-keying), which in most commercial situations is unlikely.

The majority of companies in the UK still rely very heavily on hard copy methods of storage and retrieval for competitor intelligence. Despite this, the attention they have given to the system of hard copy files is minimal. A survey of hard copy filing methods employed by a sample of UK companies, conducted by EMP Intelligence Service, found that nearly 80 per cent of competitor operations were using filing cabinets or hanging files. Only 14 per cent were using some form of ring system of filing.

Unfortunately filing cabinets or hanging files are frequently a disaster. They lack some of the key requirements for an efficient system of manual filing, in particular 'attachment'. Most material filed in twinlock files or their equivalent is unattached, and as a result is rarely in any kind of order (except when it is initially filed).

Better forms of filing involve some kind of attachment for the thinner material which can either be hole punched or placed conveniently in a 'holey plastic' and a magazine box for the thicker material. Colour coding of files makes things even easier.

This area of intelligence failure can be illustrated with two more examples drawn from consultancy experience. Company A is part of one of Europe's biggest companies in its area. The competitor intelligence operation was located in the Business Development department, and consisted largely of 12 filing cabinets. On looking inside them a colleague spotted a French language trade journal. On asking who translated it, she was told 'no-one'.

Company B is one of very few companies in its market. Watching the competition is not just desirable but essential. What it had already in the Marketing Department in terms of a competitor intelligence was neither a system, nor even a store, but a dump. Probably a thousand or more pieces of material were stored loosely in various files – a system clogged up, unproductive and moribund.

Computer filing

But however essential they may be, hard copy filing systems suffer from significant disadvantages compared with computer files, most notably their lack of speed and flexibility. Collating lists of new raw information is difficult and tedious with a hard copy system. Keeping competitor profiles up to date is also more demanding, and producing benchmarks between one's own company and competitors can become a major operation.

But software must justify its use. In particular, it must perform the following functions:

- To index and store incoming electronic information from such source types as:
  - intranet
  - Email
  - Internet
  - business information services.
- To sort both internal and external raw information to facilitate finding required pieces of information and seeing patterns in the information.
- To produce, update and communicate collations, profiles, benchmarks and analysis.

Some of these functions can be carried out by standard software, but to get them all, specialist software tailored to specific competitor intelligence needs is the answer. The basic rule about computerisation is 'Don't rush'. Think it through. Know what you want from the computer system, get your hard copy system thought out and concentrate on what may be called 'human software'.

Don't put a lot of money into computerisation and nothing into a hard copy system or into building up an internal human network. Yet do not ignore the need for the right software because computers are essential for competitor intelligence.

Synthesis/Description

> *'Dear Friend, I am sorry to send you a five page letter.*
> *I did not have time to send you a one page letter.'*
> Voltaire

The process of reducing a longer piece of raw information to a shorter one without losing the essential elements is frequently of vital importance. In the sea of information in which managers are drowning more information is not a blessing. Summaries make assimilating a larger amount of information possible. In some cases they are the difference between assimilating something or not assimilating it at all.

Producing a summary provides an opportunity to add analytical comments as well as merely cutting the number of words. Here is a humorous example for you to test your ability to summarise. Aim to produce a summary of the following – four or five words maximum.

> *Although certain broad zonational patterns are discernible in the geographical distribution of animals as well as those of soils and vegetation, the mobility of animals and, in the case of some, seasonal altitudinal migrations mean that the zonation becomes indistinct.*

This is taken from the second edition of a marvellous book: *Plain Words* by Gowers. Gowers described this piece of verbiage as: 'A mountain of words, a molehill of an idea'.

(Compare your summary with that suggested on page 156.)

Computer software, for instance Microsoft Word 97 has been developed which permits 'text summarisation'.

Forecasting/Speculation

Much of the competitor information which is received is about the recent past, or at very best current. Yet if competitor intelligence is to be really actionable, it must have a future component. This future component can sometimes be collected (e.g. a competitor's future investment strategies) but in many cases it has to be forecast or simply speculated.

Forecasting

Set out below is a brief overview of the main useful methods of forecasting. For the purposes of competitor intelligence processing, three methods of forecasting can be useful:

- Judgement
- Extrapolation
- Leading indicators.

Judgement

Judgement methods of forecasting involve asking someone for their opinion. Four such methods are:

- survey of salesforce opinion
- survey of managers opinions
- Delphi technique
- scenarios.

The first two are self-explanatory – they consist of asking the sales-force and/or selected managers for their opinions about future trends.

The Delphi technique, named after the oracle at Delphi, uses the opinions of experts via anonymous written questionnaires. The Delphi technique involves the following process:

1 Group of experts formed
2 Questionnaire sent to each expert
3 Returns analysed
4 New questionnaire. Results of first questionnaire + new questionnaire sent to experts
5 New returns analysed
6 Fresh results and new questionnaire sent.

The Delphi technique produces a range of forecasts, a range which, it is hoped, will have narrowed during the process of the technique. Some companies conduct Delphi-like exercises in discussion groups, though these exercises include the impact of group pressure whereas the pure Delphi technique tries to avoid direct contact between experts.

While the Delphi technique emphasises an anonymous step-by-step process, the emphasis of scenario technique is not on the method of forecasting but on the type of forecast itself. **A scenario** is a description of a particular pattern of a number of variables, a snapshot of the set of relationships between them, taken at a particular moment in time. Frequently, in a forecasting exercise, more than one scenario is painted for an individual time period and, in addition, scenarios can be produced for more than one period.

Extrapolation

The second method of forecasting is extrapolation of a statistical trend. Extrapolation simply means extending a trend. There are two main sorts of extrapolation: straight line and curved. Extrapolation is also used as a term to describe the forecast in such phrases as 'it's going to carry on very much as it has been doing in the past'. Extrapolation can be both quantitative and qualitative.

Leading indicators

The third forecasting method is the leading indicator. The nature of a leading indicator may be summed up as:

- a trend before a trend
- a bend before a bend.

Forecasting a competitor's performance in one area could – using the leading indicator approach – be done by identifying some other aspect of its activity which typically acts as a 'trend before a trend'. Monitoring the job advertisements of a competitor is a form of non-quantitative leading indicator forecasting.

Whatever the method of forecasting used, every forecast inevitably contains an element of gut feeling about it.

Forecasting will fill some gaps in the intelligence picture you are trying to construct, but some gaps will remain which cannot be left unfilled. These must be filled with intelligent guesswork or speculation using various methods. The main ones are:

- brainstorming
- simulation
- wargaming.

These methods can also be used to construct forecasts.

Second stage: Analysis

There are many different techniques of analysis. The particular methods you should use depend on the objectives of the intelligence operation and the nature of the raw information. A target intelligence operation will have incorporated an analytical technique in the process of building an intelligence template for presentation and reporting, and this template will reflect the specific purpose of the operation.

For instance, if the business objective is new market entry, one possible intelligence requirement might be the likely reactions of certain companies to new entry. The 'competitor reactions' template might be structured according to a number of factors affecting the likelihood, speed and strength of reaction.

Pattern of analysis

Analysis is not just a one-step process. Every intelligence operation should develop a pattern of integrated analytical techniques appropriate to the aims of the competitor operation. One such pattern of analysis is set out on Figure 5.2.

Competitive opportunities and threats

A fundamental purpose of many intelligence operations is the identification of opportunities and threats – past, current and, in particular, future. The latter includes an early warning element of future threats (e.g. new products, new competitor strategies and new competitors). For instance, a future threat could be the launch by a competitor of a new product or a change in the price of a significant competitor product or service. It could be the entry into the market of a potential competitor.

The warning of an impending threat (or opportunity) should specify the source of the threat, nature of the threat, the probability of the threat taking place and an estimate of the timing. Feeding into the opportunity and threat assessment is an analytic framework of news analysis, competitor profile analysis and strengths and weak-

Fig. 5.2 Structuring competitor intelligence to support business strategies

nesses analysis (including benchmarking analysis). The interrelationships within the analytic framework are illustrated in Figure 5.3.

Changes in competitive opportunities and threats arise from a number of causes:

● a change in the relative strengths and weaknesses between your company and certain significant competitors, caused by action taken either by competitors or by your company.

- changes in the wider competitive environment – for instance, a change in government policy or a new technology.

Assessing opportunities and threats involves the identification of current opportunities and threats, and then ranking their relative significance to the company. Forecast opportunities and threats need to be evaluated by:

- *Probability*: how certain is the forecast threat or opportunity?
- *Timing*: is the opportunity or threat forecast to occur tomorrow, in six months' or in two years' time or what?

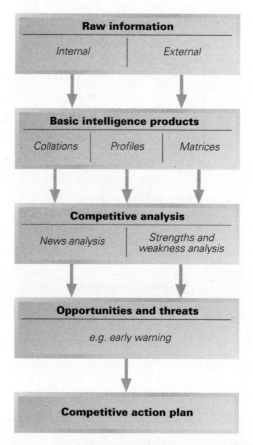

Fig. 5.3 How competitor analysis fits within the various intelligence processes

- *Effect or impact*: what will be the impact of the forecasts on the performance of the company? Good, bad or indifferent?

Of course, assessments like these are subjective, even if you have the back-up of the sophisticated quantitative forecasting techniques.

Despite their subjectivity, it is important to assess opportunities and threats in terms of these variables, as the various assumptions behind the subjective assessments can in the process be identified and discussed. One way of sharpening up these assessments is to give weights to the opportunities and threats. This is illustrated in Figure 5.4.

Forecast	Probability *1 = very unlikely* *5 = certain*	Timing *1 = LT* *2 = MT* *3 = ST*	Impact *+5 = very good* *–5 = very bad*	Total
Opportunities				
Threats				

Fig. 5.4 Analysing opportunities and threats

To begin with, the probability of something happening is weighted with a number from one to five, One stands for very unlikely and five for almost certain with levels of probability in between covered by the numbers two, three and four. Giving forecasts a ranking like this can provoke useful discussion as well as wide variations.

Timing is another variable with which to measure forecast opportunities and threats. When is the forecast event likely to happen? These can be weighted as short term, medium term and long term; which immediately begs the question: what is short, medium and long term? The answer to that question is that there is no one answer! It depends on the nature of the industry a company is in. What is short term to one industry – say, a year ahead – may be long term to another, and vice versa.

The third way in which forecast opportunities and threats may be weighted is by their probable impact or effect on the company's performance. The impact can be directly upon profitability or indirectly via price or cost competitiveness. This indirect effect on the company may therefore occur before the impact on the company's profitability.

To measure the forecast impact on the company, a scale is used, which varies from +5 at one extreme to –5 at the other.

Competitive strengths and weaknesses analysis

The standard SWOT analysis emphasises absolute strengths and weaknesses. While these are useful indicators, what frequently matter most in a competitive environment are relative strengths and weaknesses in areas that matter most to customers. A useful method of summarising strengths and weaknesses is in the form of a matrix, an example of which is illustrated in Figure 5.5.

This matrix can be used to compare the strengths and weaknesses of your company against the strengths and weaknesses of another company. There are four possible combinations.

Are you strong:

- where your competitor is strong? (Quadrant 1)
- where your competitor is weak? (Quadrant 2)

	Our company	
	Strengths	*Weaknesses*
Competitor *Strengths*	**1**	**3**
Competitor *Weaknesses*	**2**	**4**

Fig. 5.5 Strengths and weaknesses matrix

Are you weak:

● where your competitor is strong? (Quadrant 3)
● where your competitor is weak? (Quadrant 4)

Quadrant 2 is a quadrant of opportunity while Quadrant 3 is a quadrant of threat.

Relative strengths and weaknesses analysis is at the heart of competitor analysis, and there are a number of approaches one can take to carry out this form of analysis:

● competitor modelling
● value chain analysis
● key success factor analysis
● market position analysis.

A technique for evaluating forecast strengths and weaknesses is set out in Figure 5.6.

Aspect	Relative weakness			Relative strength			Importance 1 = Unimportant 5 = Very important	Total
	−3	−2	−1	+1	+2	+3		
Strength								
Weakness								

Fig. 5.6 Evaluating forecast strengths and weaknesses

Each strength and each weakness is assessed in two ways. First, how strong and how weak it is, and second how important. Importance is measured in terms of impact on profitability and competitiveness. Each of these two measures gives you a number. Multiply the two measures and you get a total which is a measure of the significance of the strength or weakness.

This method of analysis can become more useful when you forecast *future* strengths and weaknesses. Forecasts about future strengths and weaknesses may be shown on the same sort of assessment chart.

Competitive and business environment analysis

Frequently, it is useful to analyse the competitive and business environments of a competitor in order to understand the external 'drivers' acting upon its management. (This also needs to be done for one's own company).

To carry out this kind of analysis, there are a number of models you can use:

- Porter's Five Forces model
- PIMS model
- EMP model.

These are briefly described below.

Porter's Five Forces model

Michael Porter argued that the competitive pressure on a company was determined by the following forces:

- entry barriers
- rivalry
- supplier power
- buyer power
- threat of substitution.

The competitive pressure itself determines the profit potential of an industry. The 'best position' for a company can only be ascertained from an assessment of the five forces and their underlying drivers. Porter's ideas came largely from industrial structure economics, in particular the structure-conduct-performance model developed in the 1970s by such economists as F M Scherer.

PIMS model

The PIMS model considers that business performance depends on three major kinds of factors:

- the characteristics of the market in which a business competes
  - growth rate
  - entry conditions
  - purchase amounts
  - capital intensity
  - market differentiation
  - unionisation.
- the business's competitive position in that marketplace
  - relative perceived quality
  - relative market share
  - relative capital intensity
  - relative cost.
- the strategy it pursues
  - pricing
  - research and development spending
  - new product introductions
  - change in relative quality and variety of products/services
  - marketing expenses
  - distribution channels
  - relative vertical integration.

Within each of these factors, the PIMS model includes only those variables which can actually be measured quantitatively. For more information you should consult Buzzell and Gale (1987). (*See* the Bibliography on page 209.)

EMP model

This model was developed for the Open University course called *Managing in the Competitive Environment* which was published in 1987. At its simplest level it argued that there was a mutual inter-dependence between a company's external environment (**E**), the management's actions (**M**) and the company's performance (**P**). The external environment was divided into two parts: the competitive environment and the STEPP factors (see Figure 5.7).

Fig. 5.7 Structure of the business environment

The performance of a business was measured in terms of ultimate performance (profitability and competitiveness) and intermediate measures of performance (productivity, costs, etc.).

Competitor modelling/value chain

This approach consists of analysing a competitor in terms of the key components of its business in order to assess its performance and its strengths and weaknesses. Here is a model developed by EMP, which emphasises a number of interrelated aspects of a company:

- where the company is coming from
- where it appears to be going

- by what means and processes it is trying to get there
- with what results.

The model is illustrated in Figure 5.8.

Fig. 5.8 EMP competitor model

Context

This is analysed in terms of the models outlined in the last section.

Driving forces

These may be divided into external and internal driving forces. External driving forces are those external to the business – for example, pressure from external stakeholders, such as shareholders, government, institutional shareholders, brokers' analysts. Internal driving forces include the focus and individual vision of top managers. For example, one CEO of a major company in the UK is paranoid about his company being taken over and therefore resisting unwelcome attention from other companies drives much of his vision.

Objectives

Analysing the business objectives of a competitor is very important. In Figure 5.9 is a summary analysis of the perceived corporate objectives of a US company. This shows the interaction between the US company's overall objectives and those it established for penetrating the UK market.

Strategies

Marketing strategy analysis, for instance, can be carried out in a number of ways. One way is to produce a collation of competitor marketing strategy events by date, classified by price, product, added-value services, promotion, distribution and positioning, etc.

These collations will reveal insights and allow pattern analysis to be performed. Marketing strategies can also be analysed over time using the matrix in Figure 5.10, which is based on the Ansoff Matrix. This matrix is named after Igor Ansoff, the marketing guru.

This matrix can be useful for presenting the results of research into competitors' strategies. Plots can be made on the Ansoff Matrix to represent products or services and colour-coded by year of launch or re-launch. This will indicate the revealed marketing strategy of the competitor.

Performance

There are all sorts of methods of performance analysis. A standard financial one is the 'ROCE tree' which enables changes in key ratios to be analysed. (ROCE stands for 'return on capital employed'.) One such ROCE tree for a UK company is set out in Figure 5.11. The

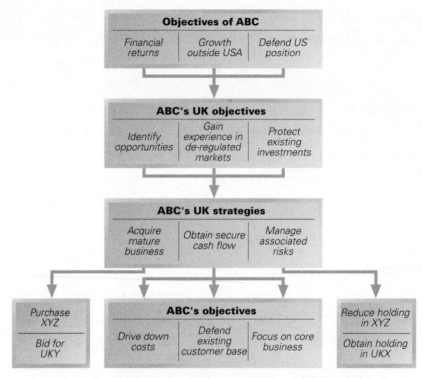

Fig. 5.9 Analysing the objectives of a US predator

| Product/Service | |
| Existing | New |

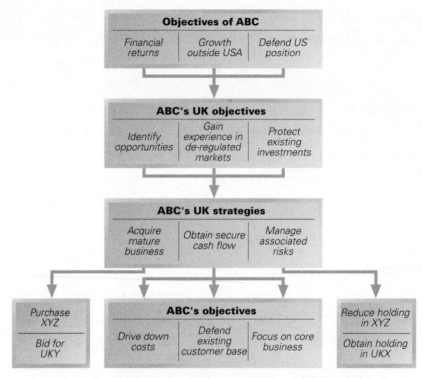

Fig. 5.10 Ansoff Matrix

figures in the boxes refer to two consecutive years, with the first of the two years printed in brackets.

The use of arrows highlights key changes. The 'tree' makes the presentation of fairly complex ratio analysis to non-financial customers much clearer. It can be associated with a bullet point analysis. One approach is set out below:

- Between 19XX and 19YY ROCE rose from 16.4 to 19.9
  - despite a lower profit margin caused by a rise in direct costs.
- ROCE rose because of a significant increase in capital productivity
  - due to a 40 per cent increase in labour productivity
  - caused by a substantial fall in the number of employees.

Other performance analysis techniques are the profitability and growth matrix and the customer satisfaction analysis (percentage of customers satisfied and importance to customers).

Value chain analysis

Value chain analysis is another way of looking at the total company, by dividing the total or some aspect of it into its key components. A simple value chain might consist of four 'links':

- Design
- Produce
- Market
- Deliver.

A slightly more detailed value chain with seven components is illustrated in Figure 5.12.

Key success factor (KSF) analysis

Key success factor analysis examines the strengths and weaknesses of a company relative to the key factors needed for success in the

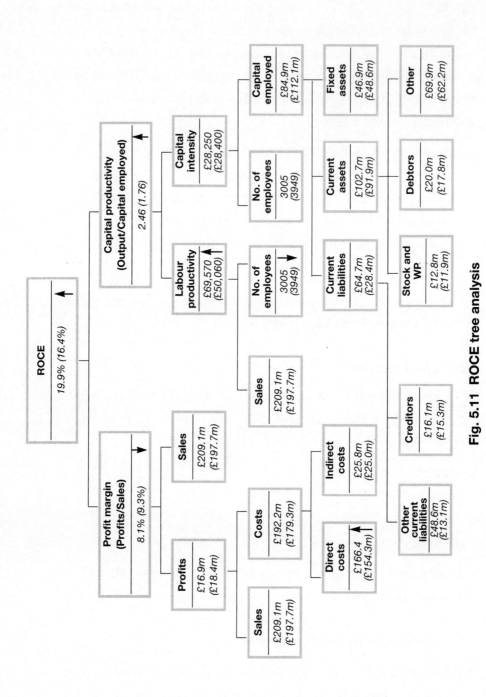

Fig. 5.11 ROCE tree analysis

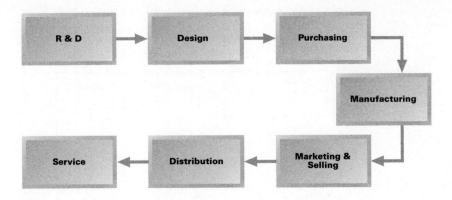

Fig. 5.12 Value chain

marketplace. For instance, a KSF competitive benchmark is illustrated in Figure 5.13.

Another technique is to analyse competitors' strengths and weaknesses (both current and forecast) against key success factors. A template for this is set out in Figure 5.14.

This template identifies what companies in a particular market *have* to do right in order to win. It then plots both current and forecast strengths and weaknesses against these key success factors. For instance, is the company strong where it needs to be or is it weak? Are its strengths likely to decline in the future and its weaknesses improve?

Market position analysis

Market position analysis examines the current and forecast position of a competitor in their key markets. There are a number of methods of market position analysis – for instance, various so-called portfolio analyses, which originally became popular in the 1960s:

- growth/share matrix (Boston Consulting Group)
- attractiveness/business position (General Electric/McKinsey)

KSF	Weight	Your company	Competitors				
			C1	C2	C3	C4	C5
	100%						

Fig. 5.13 Comparing performance against key success factors

KSF	Strengths		Weaknesses	
	Current	Forecast	Current	Forecast

Fig. 5.14 Comparing a competitor's strengths and weaknesses against KSFs

- directional policy matrix (Shell)
- industry maturity/competitive position (Arthur D Little).

These are considered in more detail below.

Boston Grid

The first is the growth/share matrix developed by the Boston Consulting Group in the USA in the 1960s and sometimes known as the 'Boston Grid'. This is illustrated in Figure 5.15.

Individual products or services and strategic units of a business can fall in any of the four quadrants, and each has a name to describe it.

Quadrant 1 is a situation of high market share in the context of high market growth. Products or services in this box are called **Stars** or **Rockets**. They are high cash generators and high cash users. Products or services in Quadrant 2 with low market share in buoyant markets and they are called **question marks** or **problem children**.

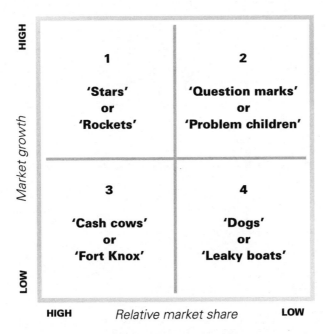

Fig. 5.15 Boston Grid

They have high cash use but lower cash generation.

In Quadrant 3 are products or services which have high market shares in markets with low growth. They are called **cash cows** or **Fort Knoxs**. Just as cows produce lots of milk, cash cows bring in lots of cash, because they are high cash generators but low cash users.

Finally, in Quadrant 4 are **dogs** or **leaky boats**. These are products or services or strategic units with low market shares in markets with low growth. Cash generation is low and so is cash use.

Individual products on the Boston Grid can be shown in the form of circles in Figure 5.16. The size of the circles reflects the size of the individual markets. The position of the circles – the centre of the circles – reflects the size of the market share on the one hand and the pace of market growth on the other.

The Boston Grid can be useful in shedding some light on the strengths and weaknesses of a competitor's products or services.

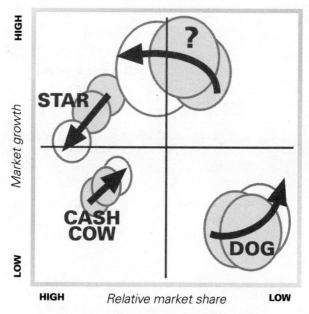

Fig. 5.16 Change in a Boston Grid

Other matrices

Another technique are the matrices developed by various companies, among them General Electric, McKinsey and Shell. The Business Assessment Array developed by General Electric and McKinsey and the Directional Policy Matrix developed by Shell have axes which measure industry attractiveness on the one hand and competitive position on the other.

The General Electric Matrix is illustrated in Figure 5.17:

	Market attractiveness		
	High	Medium	Low
Strong	1	2	3
Average	4	5	6
Weak	7	8	9

Competitive position

Fig. 5.17 General Electric Matrix

Industry attractiveness is measured by a variety of criteria:

- market size, growth and diversity
- competitive structure
- industry profitability
- STEPP factors (sociological, technological, economic, political and physical environmental).

Competitive position is in turn measured by:

- size
- growth
- market share
- profitability
- profit margins
- technological position
- image.

The nine cells in the matrix can be broken into three groups. Cells 1, 2 and 4 indicate strong positions, cells 3, 5 and 7 indicate average positions while cells 6, 8 and 9 indicate weak positions.

Suggested summary of example given on page 132:

Animals move, plants don't.

Summary of Chapter 5

- Raw information can pass through eight stages before it is communicated to an internal customer:
  - re-collection source selection/filtering
  - evaluation
  - indexing, filing and collation
  - synthesis/description
  - forecasting and speculation
  - analysis
  - production
  - communication.

- Raw information can be classified as follows:
  - checked fact
  - assumed fact
  - published material
  - rumour.

- An efficient hard copy filing system is essential for the overall efficiency of storage and retrieval.

- Summarising raw information is an important skill.

- Four methods of forecasting are commonly used:
  - judgement (e.g. Delphi, scenarios)
  - extrapolation
  - leading Indicators
  - gut feeling.

- An analytical process can be developed based on the following structure:
  - opportunities and threats
  - strengths and weaknesses:
    - competitor modelling
    - value chain analysis
    - key success factor analysis
    - market position analysis.

Troubleshooting

Common problems	How to deal with them
Stacks of hard copy items waiting for input into computer	Rationalise and prioritise input. Get as much as possible in electronic form
Vast jumble of hard copy filing based on hanging files or cabinets	Set up easy to use colour-coded ring-based system
No time for forecasting, speculation or analysis	Time management
Good intelligence not getting through to the heads of decision makers	Improve channels used and intelligence produced

6

Producing and communicating the right intelligence products

What intelligence products to produce

Specific items of evaluated raw information
Raw information collations
Competitor or target profiles
Competitor comparisons or benchmarks
Competitor analyses

Constructing the right competitor intelligence products

Choice of competitor intelligence products
Structure of individual intelligence products
Designing a good intelligence template
'Crash' analysis

Producing actionable intelligence: competitive action plans

Actionable intelligence
Competitive action plans

Communicating competitive intelligence

Effective channels of communication
Effective forms of communication
Large scale presentation of competitor information

Summary of Chapter 6

Troubleshooting

What intelligence products to produce

Managers of competitor intelligence should not think of themselves primarily as collectors or providers of information as such, but as producers of tailored intelligence *products*. Such products provide senior managers and others with essential decision support and with greater awareness of key changes in their competitive environment.

Most intelligence output falls into five basic types of intelligence product:

- specific items of raw information
- raw information collations
- competitor or target profiles
- comparisons or benchmarks
- competitor analyses.

Specific items of evaluated raw information

Managers frequently want a specific piece of information. For instance, a sales director might need to know the number of sales-people a competitor is deploying in a particular geographic region. A good competitor intelligence operation manager will find out why this piece of information is wanted and how it will be used. His/her task is to produce that figure with an evaluation of its accuracy. So, if the raw information collected is '21 in the salesforce', it will need to be checked for accuracy and timeliness.

Raw information collations

Raw information collations are assemblies of existing or new infor-mation for a particular period of time, arranged by competitor or by some other keyword. Raw information collations are one of the most commonly produced intelligence products. They are very useful for increasing awareness, for fuelling intuitive thought processes and for discerning patterns and trends. Being able to produce raw information collations depends on appropriate indexing of incoming raw information.

Competitor or target profiles

Competitor or target profiles are structured lists of collated and edited raw information about an individual company or other target (e.g. a supplier) arranged under selected headings. The headings in an individual profile should not be based on 'nice to knows' but on the intelligence requirements of customers. Profiles must be tailored, otherwise huge amounts of raw information will be collected unnecessarily.

The following profile structure should be viewed, therefore, as only a guide to some possible headings.

Background

- Where is the head office? Telephone, fax, Email and website addresses?
- Who owns the business? Any recent significant changes in ownership?
- Who runs the company? Any recent significant changes?

Driving forces/Thinking

- Why is the company the way it is? What are the main factors affecting its shape, methods of working, corporate personality, actions and performance?
- What are the driving forces pushing it on? What is its thinking? Its motives and expectations?
- What industry or market forces have moulded the company portfolio and the minds of key decision makers?

- If the target is a subsidiary of a larger company, what policy does the parent have towards the child and what do current indicators suggest will be the parent's attitude in the future?

Objectives and intentions

- Where does the company want to go? What are its plans?
- What corporate, business unit and operational objectives does the competitor have? What intentions does the competitor have, as suggested by capital expenditure, patents, trademarks and research and development activity?

Strategies

- What strategies (corporate, sales and marketing) does the company have to achieve its objectives?
- What alliances with other companies is it building?
- What cost strategies does it have?
- What are its strategies towards the 4 Ps: product, price, promotion and place?

Resources and capital

- What resources – financial material, people and intellectual – are being used to produce the products or services?
- What are the key resources the company employs to produce and market its services?
- Who are the key personnel at any level? Who makes the decisions?
- What financial resources does it have at its disposal? How deep are its pockets?
- Have there been any significant changes in recent years?

Products and services

- What products and/or services does the competitor produce? What is its product focus?
- What new products have been developed or are under development?

Key markets and customers

- Which markets does it serve? What market shares does it have in various markets or market segments? What significant changes have taken place in recent times?
- Who are its key customers? Who have they lost or gained in recent years? What was the reasons for the losses or gains?

Structure

- How is the competitor structured, functionally and geographically?
- Who are the key heads of various divisions of the company. Who makes the decisions? Where are they located?
- What is the relative importance of the various divisions? How has this importance changed in recent times?

Methods, processes and resources

- What is the company's organisational structures?
- What methods and processes are used for a decision making, b production and c distribution?

Focus, targets and timing

- What is the company's positioning and strategy?
- What is the competitor's focus concerning a products or services, b key markets and c distribution channels?
- What targets have been set? What actions has the company taken and when?

Performance

- What is the competitor's performance in terms of: financial indicators, productivity, customer service, market shares, key success factors?
- What are the competitor's costs in key areas – for example, research and development, marketing, production distribution and administration?
- What significant changes have taken place in recent years? What are the forecast trends?

Strengths and weaknesses

- What are their key strengths and weaknesses?
- What changes have taken place in recent years? For what reasons? What are the forecast trends?

The above is merely given as a guide. There is no standard list of headings which will suit all circumstances.

CASE ILLUSTRATION

Don't build mountains of competitor intelligence!

A large international food company wanted to set up a competitor intelligence operation. It decided to produce profiles on 75 competitors, each profile having ten subheadings, and these profiles were to be updated monthly. The effort in producing and updating these profiles was gigantic – a potential 9000 cell changes per month. The focus, if that is not the wrong word, was on profile production and not on decision making support.

Competitor comparisons or benchmarks

A key element of competitor intelligence is the production of two types of comparisons or benchmarks:

- competitor versus competitor
- competitor versus your business.

These comparisons can cover almost any aspect of a company's activities and performance, for instance:

- performance
  - financial
  - key success factors
- prices
- product coverage
- promotion methods
- distribution channels
- market focus
- production methods
- research and development focus.

Comparisons are made to identify vital differences both between competitors and between competitors and your company. What is vital or not is ultimately decided by customers. Where the differences are important, such comparisons reveal relative strengths or weaknesses which present themselves as competitive opportunities and threats.

Competitor analyses

These are typically short analytical frameworks for decision making, which analyse the recent past, make an assessment of the present or make a forecast of the future. Here are some examples.

News analysis

This consists of ad hoc reactive analysis of specific events. For example, news may be received which indicates that a competitor has introduced a new product. This information needs analysis to determine its importance, to assess the implications to one's own product line and to set out a framework for action in the future.

Current situation or forecast

A frequently carried out piece of competitor analysis is current situation analysis, which is produced to answer the query 'What is the competitive situation now?'. The focus of this work can vary from financial performance, market share, operational efficiency, etc.

Potential competitors early warning analysis

One piece of regular analysis which companies frequently omit to carry out is 'early warning analysis'. This highlights impending change in the competitive environment, such as a new competitor, a change in competitors' strategies, a price change, etc. In some highly dynamic markets such as banking and insurance, regularly produced forecasts of potential competitors must be carried out – not in order to produce over-reactions and competitor paranoia, but to focus attention and resources on discovering new competitors before they burst upon the scene.

Strengths and weaknesses

A vital piece of analysis which most competitor intelligence managers have to carry out *and must carry out well* is strengths and weaknesses analysis. In this analysis the essential component is *comparison*. Strengths and weaknesses analysis in competitor analysis is fundamentally relative. It is not enough to measure absolute strengths and weaknesses, but to compare your own against competitors' strengths and weaknesses or against key success factors. Strengths and weaknesses analysis will be examined in more detail later in this chapter (pages 170–3).

Competitor response analysis

Frequently, senior management is concerned with a competitor's likely reaction to some contemplated action. A useful tool for assessing likely reactions is a competitor response model which sets out the drivers affecting the reactions. This model is set out in Figure 6.1.

Figure 6.2 illustrates the relationship between the various information and intelligence products a competitive intelligence operation may provide.

Notice in Figure 6.2 how most intelligence products feed into an assessment of relative strengths and weaknesses. Unless this is done, the information collected on competitors tends to become academic and an end in itself. Such information fails the 'so what' test. That is not to say that 'background' information cannot be useful, even if it

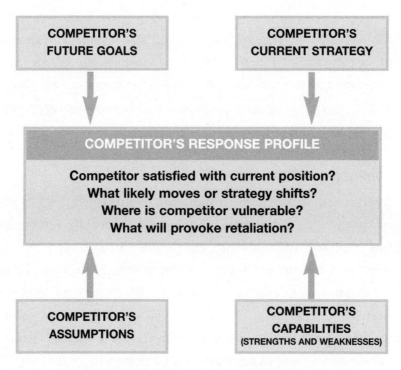

Fig. 6.1 Working out how competitors will react

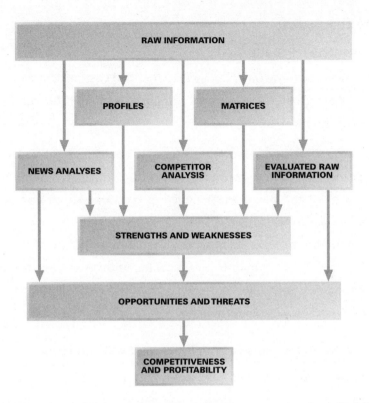

Fig. 6.2 From raw information to competitiveness and profitability

does not have immediate actionable importance. But unless a competitive intelligence operation focuses on the need to produce a return on investment in competitor intelligence, the tendency to accumulate nice-to-know information will clog the arteries of the operation.

Even strengths and weaknesses assessments are covered by these comments. They are but stepping stones – albeit important ones – towards the generation of opportunities and threats assessments, which are the basis of decision making.

Engineering company

Apart from carrying out extensive market and customer research, the Chief Executive Officer of this company wanted three additional types of intelligence:

- company profiles: economic analysis of countries in order to identify threats and opportunities and to correlate competitors' actions in the past so as to make predictions about competitor behaviour in the future
- benchmarking: non-competitive benchmarking intelligence to discover how companies in dissimilar industries but in similar market positions had succeeded – what worked and did not work
- analysis: competitive intelligence focusing on their strategies.

Strengths and weaknesses analysis and SWOT analysis

A strength your business may have is not a competitive strength unless you are stronger than a competitor. You can be strong in something but if a competitor is stronger and assuming that something is important, then the competitor has a competitive strength and you have a competitive weakness in an area that matters.

It is important, therefore, not to present absolute strengths per se but in relation to competitors' strengths and weaknesses. If you have a relative competitive strength, you have a competitive opportunity. And if you have a relative competitive weakness, then you have a competitive threat.

It is also important that a company's strengths and weaknesses are related to other opportunities and threats which may occur as a result of changes in markets or in the wider STEPP factors (e.g. as a result of changes in government policy).

A useful way of relating your company's strengths and weaknesses against competitors' strengths and weaknesses is the matrix which is illustrated in Figure 6.3. Quadrant 2 shows a situation where our company is strong and our competitor is weak. That is an area of competitive opportunity, whereas Quadrant 3 is one where we are weak and our competitor is strong. This denotes an area of competitive threat.

		Our company	
		Strengths	Weaknesses
Competitor	Strengths	1	3
	Weaknesses	2	4

Fig. 6.3 Comparing strengths and weaknesses

The analysis in Figure 6.3 is, of course, two-dimensional and excludes a third variable – importance. This emphasises the point that competitive strengths in areas of little importance need to be excluded from the analysis. One way of presenting this diagrammatically is by a three-dimensional strengths and weaknesses cube as illustrated in Figure 6.4.

A similar approach can be taken in relating a company's strengths and weaknesses to opportunities and threats. Figure 6.5 illustrates a two-dimensional strengths and weaknesses/opportunities and threats (SWOT) matrix.

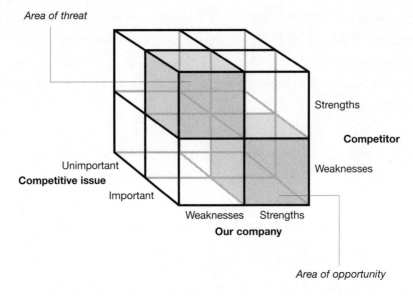

Fig. 6.4 Focusing on the important strengths and weaknesses

	(Competitor)	
	Strengths	**Weaknesses**
Opportunities		
Threats		

Fig. 6.5 Working out how competitors will react

This matrix can be compiled for your own company as well as for your key competitors. It places the strengths and weaknesses of the relevant company against market or business environmental opportunities and threats. It helps to provide answers to the questions: Does Company X have sufficient strengths to take advantage of the opportunities? Or to ward off the threats? Is it too weak to take advantage of the opportunities? Or weak enough to make it vulnerable to threats?

The three-dimensional approach illustrated in Figure 6.4 can also be used for SWOT analysis.

Constructing the right competitor intelligence products

Great care should be exercised in the choice of the competitor intelligence products you produce and in the structure and design of individual products.

Choice of competitor intelligence products

The choice of products should reflect customer needs and the resources available for competitor intelligence. If customers want competitor *information*, the products are likely to be:

- raw information
- collations of raw information
- profiles.

However, if customers prefer competitor *intelligence*, the kinds of products required are more likely to be:

- profiles
- benchmarks

- news analysis
- competitor analysis (particularly strengths and weaknesses).

Structure of individual intelligence products

The structure of a good competitor intelligence product should be based on a well-constructed intelligence template. An intelligence template is an analytic and presentational structure, or mould, into which information, filtered and assessed, is 'poured' for analysis and presentation and by which intelligence is communicated to customers. Producing a good template requires first and foremost good customer research and a willingness to test and polish the template until the internal customer is satisfied.

Good design capabilities are needed, though this should not imply that you should produce anything fancy or over-elaborate. Complicated designs rarely work and frequently reflect poor research of customers' requirements or a poor understanding of the subject matter, or both. The guidelines to follow are:

- simplicity
- clarity
- appropriateness.

Do not think that great research and even greater thinking will shine forth from a piece of intelligence and compel the reader to read it. You have to help the reader 'get the point', which is why layout, structure and choice of words/numbers/graphics are so vital. It is a sad fact, but more brilliant research languishes unread in files than is ever acted upon. To use a modern idiom, you have to 'make a statement', though that does not mean being crudely upfront about the presentation of the research.

Designing a good intelligence template

A good way of designing a template is to work backwards from the decision or decisions which need intelligence. What are the options? What kinds of analysis and implications might trigger a decision? And what kind of information would support this analysis and its implications? How could such information be analysed and presented so as to aid comprehension and decision making?

Always test a template by subjecting it to the 'so what' rule. If this intelligence product never got to the senior manager or whoever the customer happens to be, what difference would it make?

When designing a template, pay attention to details. There is so much of interest to record about competitors that it is easy to become seduced by 'nice to knows'. Every heading in a profile or a one-page competitor analysis must justify its existence. Figure 6.6 shows the basic structure of an analytical template.

The first part of the template is the header which is composed of three key elements: logo, title and date. Intelligence produced by the competitor intelligence operation should be badged in some way to say where this piece of intelligence comes from. This 'badge' might consist of the company logo, plus some reference to the name of the competitor intelligence operation. Alternatively, it might consist of a specially designed logo.

The title is obviously a key feature and should be chosen with care. It should capture interest and make the reader want to read the rest of the page. Ideally, it should make them want to know. When constructing titles, you may find the two-part title technique useful. The title is split into main heading and subheading. The main heading is the prompter, the grabber of attention, while the subheading will consist of the main question covered by the intelligence. The final part of the title is the date, usually the date the intelligence was produced.

The information block of the template sets out the information

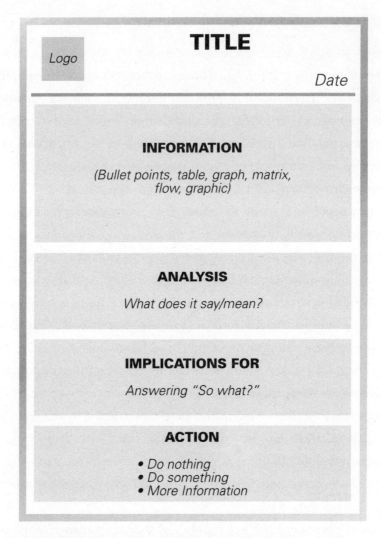

Fig. 6.6 How an analytical template is structured

relevant to the issue at hand. It can be presented in a number of ways, for instance:

- bullet points
- table
- graph

- flow diagram
- graphic.

It is frequently useful to produce the information block in two stages and in two forms. At the first stage the form includes all the information relevant to the issue, while at the second stage the information is summarised and edited to present only the key points. The first stage production should be kept as reference. It may well be used as reference material to back up the stage two product.

All too often intelligence products stop at this point, expecting senior managers to 'get the point', to do their own interpretation of the information in the information block. But the block of information should be followed by some bullet points identifying the main points. These points should then be analysed in terms of importance and relevance, highlighting important areas. It is important to put oneself into the shoes of the intelligence user and ask oneself the 'So what?' question. Your intelligence product should clearly answer the question, 'Why are you telling me this?'

The last part of an intelligence template consists of some recommendations about the next steps. In generic terms there are three broad options open to a decision maker:

- Do nothing
- Collect more information
- Do something.

For instance, you may receive a rumour about a competitor introducing a new product. This rumour is assessed as important and potentially significant to your company. But it still remains a rumour, so the appropriate action will probably be to collect more information seeking to confirm or refute the rumour.

A frequently useful template is the matrix template in which the information block is made up of a comparison between your company and a competitor company or companies. It is useful for comparing financials, prices and other numbers or short word summaries. A basic example is illustrated in Figure 6.7.

CASE ILLUSTRATION

Joint venture or merger opportunities

A finance company set itself the target of being in the top 15 finance companies in the world by the year 2000. Organic growth alone was not going to enable it to achieve that target. It was essential to boost growth either by a joint venture or by a merger.

The company set up a competitor intelligence operation partly to help it gather 'growth by acquisition' opportunities. Part of their operation consisted of a sophisticated and detailed product comparison between the finance company and its competitors. This particular tool had the dual advantage of being useful both at a strategic and tactical level. One important variation of the matrix template is the salesforce intelligence template. The information block sets out some relevant comparisons, while the action points below the block can focus on the selling implications of the information.

The content of the various templates which a competitor intelligence manager develops should drive the competitor intelligence operation, as Figure 6.8 illustrates. For these templates are more than just output vehicles. They are the form of contract which binds intelligence producer to intelligence user. Another way of looking at these templates is to think of them as products produced for a customer (as indeed they are). They reflect requirements, they drive collection and they determine the processes of intelligence analysis and production.

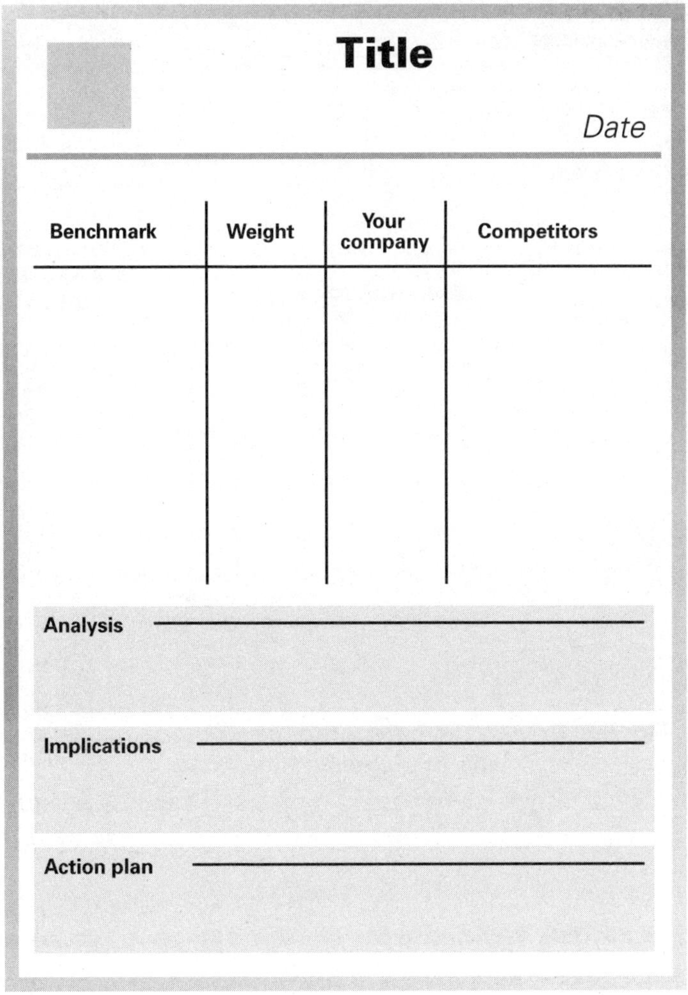

Title

Date

Benchmark	Weight	Your company	Competitors

Analysis ————————————————————

Implications ————————————————————

Action plan ————————————————————

Fig. 6.7 Matrix template

'Crash' analysis

Even well ordered and carefully set up competitor intelligence operations need occasionally to carry out 'crash' analysis on newly
emerging competitors or on topics hitherto considered unimportant. 'I want an analysis of their strategy and I want it in three hours!'
is the message that can strike fear and trembling in the hearts of any
competitor intelligence manager. So how to do it well and quickly?

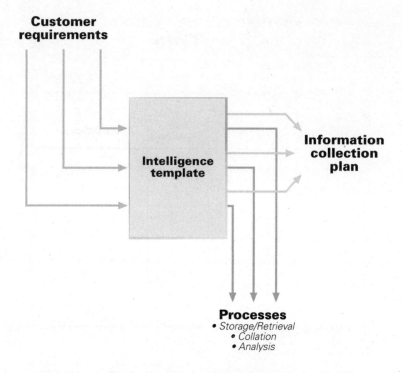

Fig. 6.8 Driving the competitor intelligence operation with intelligence templates

Here is a Crash Analysis paper based action plan. A similar computer based action plan can be developed.

Purpose   Analysing a mass of hard copy information to identify the competitor's product/service strategy

Raw information 100+ sheets of database printout, Internet output and a couple of competitor brochures

Tools needed Highlighters of different colours + coloured pens

Mental process Decide which of the following questions are crucial to your analysis:

- What?
- Who?
- Why?
- Where?
- How?
- When?

Let us say that one of the crucial questions is: *What products/services* have been launched in *what markets* and *when*?

Each of these three questions is allocated a different coloured highlighter and the raw material is then read at some speed and marked up with these highlighters. A simple three-column table can then be constructed – when, what markets and what products/services. This could be the basis of the information block or the basis of information to be inserted into the matrix based on the Ansoff Matrix which was examined on pages 147–9.

Variations of this simple process have produced an astonishingly good analysis from fairly raw and rough information in as little as 90 minutes.

Producing actionable intelligence: competitive action plans

Actionable intelligence

The end product of a competitor intelligence operation is actionable intelligence – intelligence upon which action can be based. A competitive action plan identifies what should be done, when, by whom and by what deadline.

Fig 6.9 From information to a competitive action plan

Competitive action plans

Competitive action plans (CAPs) formulate the action to be taken based on intelligence produced. CAP is a generic term. In reality it may be called a marketing plan, sales plan, key account plan, etc. Such action may be directed at changing some part of the internal workings of the business, such as improving the selling procedure, reducing production costs, increasing efficiency or changing the way things should be organised. Alternatively, a CAP may be more concerned with externally orientated change, for instance:

- increasing sales, e.g. by product/service differentiation and new products or by entering new markets,
- buying a competitor, i.e. reduce competition and buy market share
- collaborating with a competitor, e.g. by licensing, marketing agreements, research, joint ventures or franchising
- quitting a market
- reducing competition by building barriers or making competition more difficult or more expensive
- increase competition, e.g. price or other changes in the offer package
- improving relations with a customer.

In assessing the potential benefit of any particular CAP, it is important to consider each CAP in terms of positives to the company and also negatives to the competition.

Competitor intelligence, whether radar awareness or target intelligence, can only benefit a company when it influences action in a beneficial way, or when it sensibly supports a decision to do nothing. Doing nothing instead of doing something is a perfectly valid option, as long as it is consciously and appropriately done.

Not all pieces of raw information collected will themselves be actionable. They may merely end up as part of a profile. Even so, they should contribute to the production of actionable intelligence.

The proportion of actionable intelligence which is produced relative to raw information collected is important to monitor to avoid amassing vast amounts of non-actionable competitor information.

CASE ILLUSTRATIONS

Competitive action plan

Identify premium price opportunities

A manufacturer was faced with a declining market realised that one way of maintaining and even increasing profitability was to identify opportunities to charge premium prices. It did this by looking for situations where the level of competition was lower than average and where the manufacturer had a relative advantage over their competitors. This they did to such advantage that their sales were increased by over £1m.

Reduce competitors' prices

A key objective of reducing competitors' prices is to reduce their margins and thereby reduce their profitability. One of the purposes is to drive the competitor out of business or to damage or to scare the competitor into reducing or eliminating certain competitive acts.

Consider the example of a multinational company with its headquarters in the southern hemisphere. It had begun to suffer competition in its own country from European companies. So it collected intelligence to identify where and how to retaliate to best advantage.

Based on this intelligence, the multinational entered certain competitor's own home markets with very low prices. The competitors got the message!

Communicating competitor intelligence

The task of a competitor intelligence manager is not complete until the information that has been collected and processed has been communicated effectively to the relevant internal customer. But what does 'communicated effectively' mean?

Effectiveness involves consideration of:

- what you are trying to communicate
- how the customer prefers information to be received in terms of channel and form.

Effective channels of communication

The main channels of communication are:

- voice
  - personal face-to-face meeting with end user
  - audio/video tape sent to end user
  - video link
  - presentation by third party
- hard copy
  - back-up to face-to-face presentation
  - internal mail
- electronic
  - Email or intranet
  - disk.

Two of the best methods of communicating competitor intelligence to customers are:

- personal oral delivery to the end user
- customised reports (hard copy or electronic) based on clearly constructed templates.

If you are making a presentation, concentrate your presentation on what is really important. Imagine you have only one OHP to make your presentation and your audience have only five minutes to absorb your presentation and ask questions. Alternatively, imagine you can only communicate by audio tape and your listener/customer is driving in heavy traffic.

Effective forms of communication

A piece of information may be communicated in a number of different forms.

- words/bullet points
- numbers (e.g. percentages)
- tables/graphs/benchmarks
- matrices (e.g. SWOT matrix)
- graphics (e.g. value chain)
- pyramid chart (e.g. for financial ratios)
- other charts (e.g. cash flow diagram).

Designing the right template to convey a particular piece of information to a certain person is therefore partly art, partly technique and largely a good deal of experience. Take cash flow, for instance. An analysis of a competitor's cash flow can be presented in a variety of forms:

- table
- flow chart (in and out)

- bar chart
- bullet points.

Which you choose depends on the channel of communication, as well as on the preferences of the customer. Whether the channel is hard copy or electronic, there are no rigid rules for choosing the best forms for communicating competitor intelligence. It is a matter of 'horses for courses'. Apart from the ubiquitous sentences/bullet points and tables and graphs, a number of other forms of presentations can be useful.

Large-scale presentation of competitor information

One example is large-scale presentation. There are some distinct advantages in being able to see at a glance all aspects of a competitor intelligence project. This can usually only be done in a secure way by setting aside a room (sometimes called the 'war room') where the various informational and intelligence components of a project may be displayed on the walls.

A useful design is to erect movable panels on rails which enables individual panels to be moved at will. Figure 6.10 illustrates a basic design.

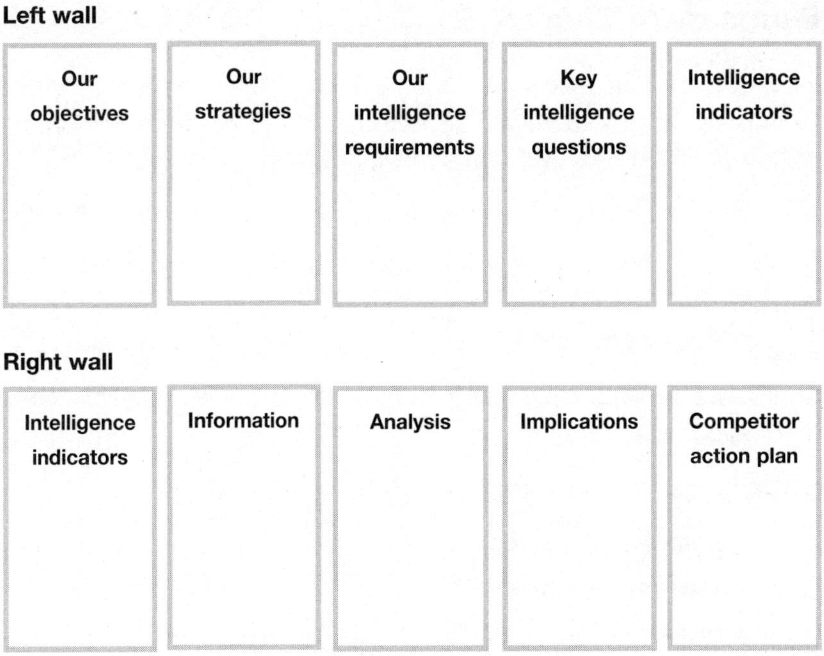

Left wall

Our objectives	Our strategies	Our intelligence requirements	Key intelligence questions	Intelligence indicators

Right wall

Intelligence indicators	Information	Analysis	Implications	Competitor action plan

Fig. 6.10 'War room' panels

Summary of Chapter 6

- A good deal of intelligence output falls into the following types:
    - pecific items of evaluated raw information
    - raw information collations
    - competitor or target profiles
    - competitor versus competitor comparisons
    - competitor analyses.

- The pattern of intelligence products will (or should) reflect intelligence requirements.

- An analytical template will consist of four components:
    - information (structured)
    - analysis of the information
    - implications
    - action.

- The end product of a competitive intelligence operation is actionable intelligence.

- Intelligence should be communicated in the most appropriate and effective manner.

Troubleshooting

Common problems	How to deal with them
Competitive intelligence manager does not have enough time to produce everything that is wanted	Get more resources or rationalise production
Senior managers don't have enough time to read all that is produced	Change content and design to improve chances of intelligence being assimilated by senior managers
Intelligence produced lacks actionable quality	Take intelligence to the point where it contains actionable element

7

Security and ethics

Security and leaks

Identify critical intelligence
Identify potential leaks
Reduce risk

Ethics

How far do people go when collecting competitor intelligence?
So what can we do about it?
SCIP code of ethics

The role of government in competitor intelligence

*Governments as preventers of illegal intelligence collection
    methods*
*Governments as practitioners of normally illegal intelligence
    methods*

Summary of Chapter 7

Troubleshooting

Security and leaks

The previous six chapters have shown how a competitor intelligence operation can make a significant contribution to business objectives. Unfortunately, the benefits of such investment can be substantially reduced by the lack of good security.

For every atom of benefit gained from producing competitor intelligence another atom may be lost through inadequate security. So every potential leak of information which is plugged represents an addition to the bottom line of competitor intelligence. The basic steps in competitor intelligence security are:

- Identify critical intelligence.
- Identify potential leaks.
- Reduce risk.

Each of these is considered below.

Identify critical intelligence

The first step to protecting your secrets is to identify what they are. Among the most critical items of corporate information which needs to be protected are:

- customer lists
- pricing data
- production development/unique or exceptional manufacturing process
- research and development secrets (plans, activities, inventions)
- sales data
- manufacturing process information
- costing data (e.g. R&D and production)
- marketing strategies (e.g. new product introduction plans and timing)

- strategic business plans
- financial statements
- factory blueprints, floor plans and layouts
- waste/garbage.

Identify potential leaks

The second step is to identify potential leaks. To do this, you should build up an information map for your company. Identify what information about your company flows out of the company, how and where it flows out and when it flows out. There are four main flows:

- downstream (customers, brokers, dealers, distributors and retailers)
- upstream (suppliers, consultants, advertising agencies and, contract services)
- government
- private stakeholders (community groups, special interest groups, press, brokers and analysts).

Company secrets leak out in a variety of ways:

- speeches and trade shows
- staff who love to gossip
- Email/web pages
- exhibitions and conferences
- publications
- plant and factory tours
- industry studies
- customers
- suppliers
- business partners
- government disclosures
- staff with a grudge (e.g. ex-staff).

Reduce risk

You have identified your key secrets and assessed how 'leaky' you are. The next step is to stop up the potential leaks of crucial information.

The best ways of protecting competitor information are:

- Educate employees.
- Build and maintain security awareness.
- Create structured processes for identifying "intelligence attacks" on your company.
- Establish teams to manage responsibility for competitor intelligence.
- Build and maintain relationships with non-employees who know secrets and ex-employees who know secrets.
- Audit the company's protection performance periodically.

Ethics

Competitor intelligence is not industrial espionage. The latter uses illegal means to obtain competitors' secrets, while the former emphasises its legal credentials. Nothing included in this book can be construed as illegal. That is not to say that in practice only strictly ethical means are always used to collect competitor information, and readers need to be aware of some of the methods employed by potential and actual competitors in an 'intelligence attack' on their company.

How far do people go when collecting competitor intelligence?

What methods are actually used to collect information on competitors? Probably the biggest survey on research behaviour in competitor intelligence has been the survey EMP Intelligence Service has carried out since 1989 based on 3500 attendees to its public seminars, largely from the UK.

Some of the key findings, based on a sample of about 660 attendees, are set out below. Attendees were given a list of methods of collecting competitor information and asked to mark those methods which they were either willing to use or had already used. The questionnaires were unmarked and delegates' names were not recorded on the questionnaires.

Their responses are grouped under three main headings:

- common practice
- fairly common
- uncommon and illegal practices.

Common practice

The following are each carried out by more than 50 per cent of respondents:

- Putting camouflaged questions to competitors' employees at technical or other meetings: 78 per cent
- Questioning competitors' employees attending job interviews at own company: 66 per cent
- Positioning oneself in order to overhear a conversation between competitors' employees: 65 per cent
- Taking exterior photographs/video of competitors' plant/building works/office: 52 per cent
- Calling competitors' suppliers and distributors pretending to do a study of the entire industry: 55 per cent
- Posing as a student working on a thesis: 51 per cent

The first four may be classed as taking advantage of opportunities, while the last two move into the grey area of deception. Nevertheless, as you can see, these methods are very common.

Fairly common

The following are each carried out by between 25–50 per cent of respondents:

- Hiring an employee away from a competitor in order to obtain specific information or know-how: 44 per cent
- Paying a consultant who has worked for a competitor for information: 39 per cent
- Giving a competitor's employee a job interview simply to get information out of him/her: 31 per cent
- Hiring a professional investigator to obtain a specific piece of information: 29 per cent
- Going to a job interview at a competitor simply to get information: 28 per cent
- Entering into negotiations with a competitor for a licence in order to obtain secret information: 25 per cent
- Paying a retired employee of a competitor for information: 23 per cent

Most of the above are 'grey' areas and involve deception.

Uncommon and illegal practices

- Entering a competitor's building site without permission: 8 per cent
- Using electronic means to overhear conversations: 3 per cent

Bugging does not seem to be very common (though one person in 30 would use the technique), but one person in 12 would trespass on competitors' land.

So what can we do about it?

These findings are probably not much of a surprise, but they should add weight to the need for security. Here are some action points which arise:

- Watch what you say to competitors at technical or chance meetings.
- All staff going to competitors for job interviews should be briefed beforehand and debriefed afterwards.
- Even if you are talking only to colleagues of your own company at technical meetings at which competitors are present, again watch what you say.
- All calls to the company by researchers doing 'an industry survey' and by students should be routed through a central point. A log should be kept and proof of college affiliation should be requested.
- Monitor job advertisements by competitors and try to ensure all staff report any interviews they are going to (not always easy).
- Any staff in contact with competitors must be briefed about being tight-lipped.
- Keep in touch with ex-employees. Try to keep them loyal to the company or at least know where those still in work have gone. Encourage selected ex-staff to report any approaches for information about your company.

SCIP code of ethics

The US-based Society of Competitor Intelligence Professionals (SCIP) has done a great deal in developing conferences and knowledge of tools, techniques and best practice. Part of its statement of purpose is to 'advocate high ethical standards for the profession', and to this purpose SCIP includes the following code of ethics in their publications:

- To strive continually to increase respect and recognition for the profession.
- To pursue one's duties with zeal and diligence while maintaining

the highest degree of professionalism and avoiding all unethical practices.

- To adhere faithfully to and abide by one's company's policies, objectives and guidelines.
- To comply with all applicable laws.
- To disclose all relevant information accurately, including one's identity and one's organisation, prior to all interviews.
- To respect fully all requests for confidentiality of information.
- To promote and encourage full compliance with these ethical standards within one's company, with third party contractors and within the entire profession.

These are, of course, very laudable aims, but how far SCIP can enforce them or even know if they are being breached is debatable. In truth, there is not much that SCIP, or any other voluntary organisation, can do to find out what is really going on. Even if it did find out, how far could it ensure standards are raised, let alone be enforced?

But this lack of ability to enforce ethical standards should not necessarily reflect badly on voluntary organisations such as SCIP. If governments cannot altogether or even largely prevent the use of, say, deception or the practice of economic espionage in competitor intelligence, what chance have organisations like SCIP which lack legal muscle?

The role of government in competitor intelligence

This is not the place for an extensive discussion of the role played (or should be played or should not be played) by government in competitor intelligence. Suffice to say that so far governments around the world appear to be acting in three different ways, each of which will affect the perception and growth of competitor intelligence as a significant component of modern management practice.

These roles may be summarised as follows:

- Government as a preventer of illegal intelligence collection methods – laws to punish economic espionage.
- Government as an employer of legal intelligence collection methods – e.g. 'open source' collection (not discussed below).
- Government as an employer of normally illegal intelligence collection methods – e.g. communications interception and monitoring.

Some governments appear to be playing the roles of both regulators and practitioner of illegal operations at the same time!

Governments as preventers of illegal intelligence collection methods

Governments are naturally very keen to defend domestic companies from illegal intelligence attacks from foreign companies or governments. For instance, in October 1996 the USA enacted The Economic Espionage Act which gave the federal government the power to institute proceedings against individuals and organisations who knowingly steal, misappropriate or convert a company's trade secrets or intellectual property.

The term 'trade secret' means all forms and types of financial, business, scientific, technical, economic or engineering information, including software and computer codes, whether tangible or intangible which a company can reasonably show was treated as a trade secret.

The Act applies to conduct in the USA and outside the USA if the accused is a citizen of the USA or if the act in question was carried out in furtherance of an offence commited in the USA. If the alleged offence is carried out on behalf of a foreign government penalties are very much more severe.

Governments as practitioners of normally illegal intelligence collection methods

Governments may find it tempting to intervene in the market system in order to gain a competitive advantage for some companies in their country. They can do this directly by using some of the massive national intelligence operations they have under their control, and which were originally built up in response to Soviet or terrorist threats. These government-run intelligence operations may employ collection methods which would, if carried out by private consultancies, be deemed illegal. Governments may also intervene indirectly by working through private consultancies or trade associations as 'fronts'.

The extent to which governments are using either direct or indirect, legal or illegal methods of commercial intelligence gathering cannot largely be ascertained and there is little benefit in speculating here, though the extent to which foreign governments are targetting domestic companies is of importance in many countries.

But, for most companies, these aspects of government activities are beyond their 'need to know'. Instead, their competitive intelligence requirements will be well satisfied by the legal processes set out in this book.

Summary of Chapter 7

- The benefits of producing competitor intelligence can be out-weighed by the losses from poor security.

- The basic principle of good security is 'Don't leak important information'.

- Improving security involves three steps:
  - Identify critical intelligence.
  - Identify potential leaks.
  - Reduce risk.

- The likelihood of suffering a particular form of 'intelligence attack' varies according to the method used. Some methods are very commonly used. Some illustrations follow:

Method(s)	Chance
Camouflaged questions to your staff at meetings	8 out of 10
Questions to your employee at an interview with competitor	7 out of 10
Competitors positioning themselves to overhear your conversation with a colleague	7 out of 10
Competitor calls your suppliers and distributors pretending to do a study of an entire industry	5 out of 10
Competitor calls your company pretending to be a student doing a thesis	5 out of 10

Troubleshooting

Common problems	How to deal with them
Security slack or non-existent	Produce competitor intelligence rules and get them endorsed by senior managers
Continuous leaks from senior managers, website and PR	Educate senior managers on potential losses and introduce security rules
Company open to 'industry surveys' and 'student' attack	Centralise all requests. Filter them rigorously or ban them altogether
Managers 'spilling the beans' at conferences	Enforce strict guidelines regarding conference presentations

Glossary

Analysis One or more processes which add value to a particular piece or pieces of competitor information. Useful processes are:

- pre-collection selection/filtering
- evaluation
- indexing/filing and collation
- synthesis/description
- forecasting/speculation
- opportunities and threats
- strengths and weaknesses
- competitive environment analysis
- competitor modelling
- key success factor analysis
- market position analysis.

Analytical framework The particular pattern of analytical processes which is constructed to support a particular intelligence strategy.

Collection plan A statement of the sources to be tapped in order to collect particular information, how those sources are to be tapped, by whom and by what deadline.

Competitive action plan The *raison d'être* for a competitor intelligence operation. A statement of what action should be taken in response to intelligence produced about competitors.

Competitive advantage Relative advantage over competitors in key areas.

Competitive intelligence Information about the past, current or forecast situation or actions of past, current or future customers, competitors, suppliers and markets, which has received some form of processing or analysis.

Competitor analysis One or more analytical processes applied to a piece of competitor information.

Competitor information Information about competitors that has not yet been evaluated, or in any other way been processed into intelligence. (Sometimes called 'raw' competitor information.)

Competitor intelligence Information about the past, current or forecast situation or about the actions of competitors, which has received some form of processing or analysis. In short, competitor intelligence is 'added value' competitor information.

Competitor intelligence failure Significant ignorance of important elements of a business's competitive environment, or of changes in important aspects, which result in serious deterioration in the performance of the business.

EMP model A model which analyses a company's performance as an interaction between business strategy and significant elements of the external environment of the business.

External environment The total external context of a business, which is made up of:

- Competitive environment
  - market
  - customers
  - suppliers
- STEPP factors.

External sources Sources of competitor intelligence which exist outside your own company. These sources may be human (e.g. a customer or supplier), hard copy (e.g. brochures or reports), electronic (e.g. commercial databases or the Internet) and other (e.g. competitors' products).

Filtering The process of reducing the raw information collected to manageable proportions or restricting the information actually received by pre-collection filtering.

'Head' intelligence Information about competitors which is largely or wholly in the minds of certain key individuals, either inside or outside your company.

Intelligence indicators Competitor behaviour in certain areas which signals or indicates probable action by a competitor in areas of interest.

Intelligence template The structure, content and design of an intelligence product.

Internal network A number of selected individuals inside your company who have been encouraged to become valuable ongoing sources of competitor information.

Internal sources Sources of competitor intelligence which exist within your own company. These sources may be human, hard copy (e.g. reports), electronic (e.g. files) and other (e.g. competitors' products).

Key intelligence questions Key intelligence requirements broken down into individual components.

Key intelligence requirements Competitor intelligence needs of a customer, frequently expressed as an initial imprecise request.

Key success factor analysis Comparison of the performance of competitors with that of your own company in specific areas which consumers/external customers have stated are key to their purchase or re-purchase of the product or service in question.

PIMS model A model which sets out to explain which quantitatively measureable factors are significant in their positive or negative impact on the performance of a business.

Radar intelligence Information about competitors collected by the ongoing monitoring of selected aspects of selected competitors which has received some form of processing or analysis. Also called ongoing awareness intelligence.

Raw information Information as it has been received before any form of analysis has been carried out.

Raw information collation A compilation of raw or partly analysed information selected by particular criteria and arranged by competitor, date, subject, etc.

STEPP factors Sociological, technological, economic, political and physical environment factors external to a business and which have had, are having or could have a significant impact on the business.

Tailored intelligence Competitor information which has been processed and analysed individually for a particular customer.

Target intelligence One-off collection and evaluation of information about specific aspects of specific competitors collected in support of the formulation or execution of a particular strategy.

Third party sources Any sources of competitor information which are not inside your own company nor inside the competitor company.

Total intelligence Intelligence produced on the past, current and forecast state of a business's external environment. Its main components are:

- market intelligence
- customer intelligence
- competitor intelligence
- supplier intelligence
- STEPP intelligence.

Select bibliography

Rather than an exhaustive bibliography on competitor intelligence, this is a short list of books which readers may find useful in their reading.

Christopher Andrew, *For the President's Eyes Only* (London: HarperCollins, 1995)

Robert D Buzzell and Bradley T Gale, *The PIMS Principles: Linking Strategy to Performance* (New York: The Free Press, 1987)

Henry C Clausen and Bruce Lee, *Pearl Harbor Final Judgement* (New York: Crown, 1992)

Leonard M Fuld, *The New Competitor Intelligence* (New York: John Wiley, 1995)

Benjamin Gilad and Tamar Gilad, *Business Intelligence System: A New Tool for Competitive Advantage* (New York: Amacom, 1988)

Ben Gilad and Jan P Herring (Editors), *The Art and Science of Business Intelligence Analysis* (Greenwick, JAI Press, 1996)

Ernest Gowers, *The Complete Plain Words*, 2nd edition (London, HMSO, 1973)

Larry Kanaher *Competitive Intelligence: How to Gather, Analyse and Use Information to Move your Business to the top* (New York, Simon & Schuster, 1996)

John McGonagle and Carolyn M Vella, *A New Archetype for Competitive Intelligence* (Westport: Quorum Books, 1996)

Keith Neilson and B J C McKercher (Editors), *Go Spy the Land: Military Intelligence in History* (Westport, Praeger, 1992)

James J Weitz, *The Tet Offensive: Intelligence Failure in War* (Ithaca, Cornell Unversity Press, 1991)

John Winton, *Ultra at Sea* (London: Leo Cooper, 1988)

Index